The Explorers
Charting the Canadian Wilderness

Ernest Langford

General Editors
Carol Langford
Chuck Heath

Teacher Consultants
Vicki Mulligan
Pamela Thomas

Explorations A Canadian Social Studies Program for Elementary Schools

Douglas & McIntyre (Educational) Ltd.
1615 Venables Street
Vancouver, British Columbia V5L 2H1

Canadian Cataloguing in Publication Data

Langford, Ernest, 1920–
The explorers

(Explorations : a Canadian social studies program
for elementary schools. Exploring Canada's past)
Includes index.
ISBN 0-88894-866-2

1. Canada — Discovery and exploration — Juvenile
literature. 2. Indians of North America — Canada —
Juvenile literature. 3. Explorers — Biography —
Juvenile literature. I. Title. II. Series.
FC179.L36 1984   917.1'04   C84-091036-3
F1027.5.L36 1984

Printed and bound in Canada.

A Message from the Author

Have you ever been out walking and found a new path? And have you followed it to see where it would go? Have you ever stood on the bank of a river? And have you wondered where it would take you? Maybe you have looked at a mountain and said, "One day I'll climb that mountain and find out what is on the other side."

If you have done any of these things, then you have had the itch to be an explorer. The itch to follow unknown paths, to travel along unknown rivers and to cross unknown mountains is what exploring is all about. It means going to new places. It means finding out what they are like and how the people there live.

In this book, you will follow the journeys of explorers who came to Canada long ago. They came from Europe to explore an unknown land. This book is about the dangers the explorers faced. It is also about their triumphs.

This book is part of Canada's story. It is also part of your story.

We wish to thank the following people, who reviewed parts of the manuscript or illustrations, for their helpful comments and suggestions:

A. McFadyen Clark, Chief, Canadian Ethnology Service, National Museum of Man, Ottawa

Dr. Hugh Dempsey, Assistant Director (Collections), Glenbow Museum, Calgary

Dr. Robin Fisher, Professor, Department of History, Simon Fraser University

Verna Kirkness, Director, Native Indian Teacher Education Program, University of British Columbia

Dr. Jack Little, Associate Professor, Department of History, Simon Fraser University

Peter L. Macnair, Curator of Ethnology, British Columbia Provincial Museum, Victoria

Dr. Edward S. Rogers, Chairman, Department of Ethnology, Royal Ontario Museum, Toronto

Dr. Allen Seager, Assistant Professor, Department of History, Simon Fraser University

Hilary Stewart, author, whose books include *Indian Fishing, Looking at Indian Art of the Northwest Coast* and *Cedar*

Lorna Williams, former curriculum development program director at Mount Currie

CONTENTS

1

Who Were the First Explorers in Canada?

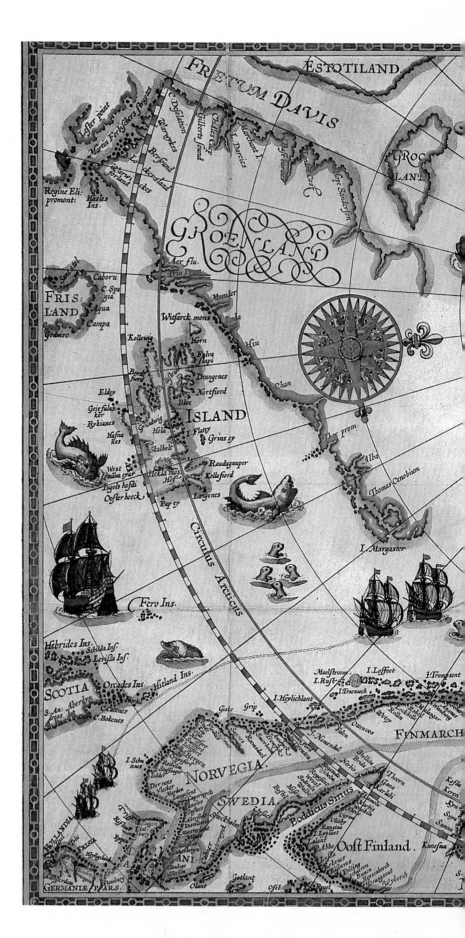

Early explorers did not know what the earth looked like. This is what one early mapmaker thought the northern part of the earth looked like.

6

The Inuit and the Indians Come to Canada

Long ago, there were no people living in the land we now call Canada. Then, thousands of years ago, the first people came to our country. Today these people are known as the Inuit and the Indians. They are Canada's native people.

Some people think that the native people came across the Bering Strait from Asia in small groups of hunters. The Inuit stayed in the north, along the shores of the Arctic Ocean. There they hunted seals and caught fish. Gradually the Inuit moved east, all the way across the Arctic.

The Indians hunted musk oxen and caribou. As they followed the herds, the Indians slowly moved south and east across the country. Some Indians lived in the forest, and some lived on the grasslands called **prairies**. Others stayed by the ocean. Many settled along the lakes and rivers. Eventually the Indians settled all across Canada.

The native people were Canada's first explorers. They lived here for a long time before anyone else came to this country.

Why do you think the Inuit and the Indians crossed the Bering Strait from Asia?

The Inuit and the Indians probably came across the Bering Strait from Asia. How might they have travelled?

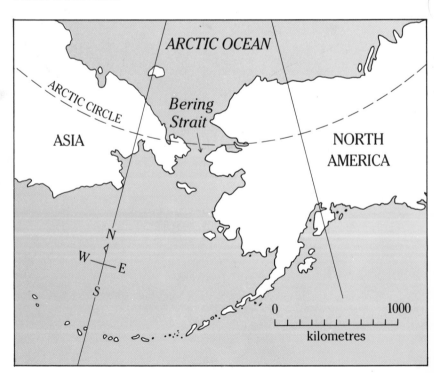

8

An Indian artist painted this picture of some of the Indians who lived on the prairies. What can you tell about their way of life?

People from Europe Come to Canada

On the other side of the Atlantic Ocean, people in Europe did not know anything about Canada. No one from Europe had ever crossed the ocean. Long ago people looked at the ocean much as we look at outer space today. The Atlantic Ocean was unknown and frightening. People thought that sailors who went too far from land would be swallowed by monsters. They thought that ships would fall off the edge of the earth.

The Legend of Saint Brendan

Saint Brendan and some other monks are in their leather boat. Why is the boat on top of a large fish?

We don't know when the first person from Europe crossed the Atlantic Ocean. There is a **legend** that a monk sailed across the Atlantic 1400 years ago. The monk was Saint Brendan. He sailed from Ireland with some other monks in a small boat made out of leather. They were looking for new lands. Saint Brendan said that he and the other monks saw **icebergs** on their journey. He also said they landed on the back of a whale. They thought the whale was an **island**.

Recently some young men who lived in Ireland decided to find out if they could cross the Atlantic in a leather boat. They built a boat like Saint Brendan's and set out over the great Atlantic waves. It was a long, hard journey. At last the little boat landed on the shores of Newfoundland.

The young men proved that it is possible to sail across the Atlantic in a boat made of leather. Still, we cannot be sure that the story of Saint Brendan is true. His daring crossing of the Atlantic remains a legend.

Why would it be hard to sail across the ocean in a small boat?

The Voyages of the Vikings

The Vikings were people who lived in the countries we call Norway, Sweden and Denmark today. They sailed across the Atlantic Ocean in wooden ships called knorrs. Over 1000 years ago, the Vikings discovered Iceland and settled there. Later a Viking called Erik the Red and some of his friends sailed west from Iceland to Greenland. When they got to Greenland, they built houses and settled down to live there.

Erik the Red had a son called Leif the Lucky. One day a young Viking who had been lost in a storm told Leif he had seen land far to the west of Greenland. Leif and some of his friends sailed off in a knorr to explore the new land.

The first land Leif found was covered with **glaciers** and flat rocks. Leif and his men did not like the look of this land and sailed on to the south. After a while they saw land that was covered with trees. The Vikings continued sailing. At last they came to a wide **bay**. The Vikings landed on the beach and walked through meadows where the grass was so long it almost reached their waists. They saw streams and lakes filled with trout and salmon. Everywhere the Vikings walked they found beautiful trees, flowers and berries. Because the berries looked like grapes, Leif named the new country Vinland.

This map shows the area that Brendan and the Vikings explored. Which are the countries where the Vikings lived?

How do you think the Vikings felt when they found Vinland?

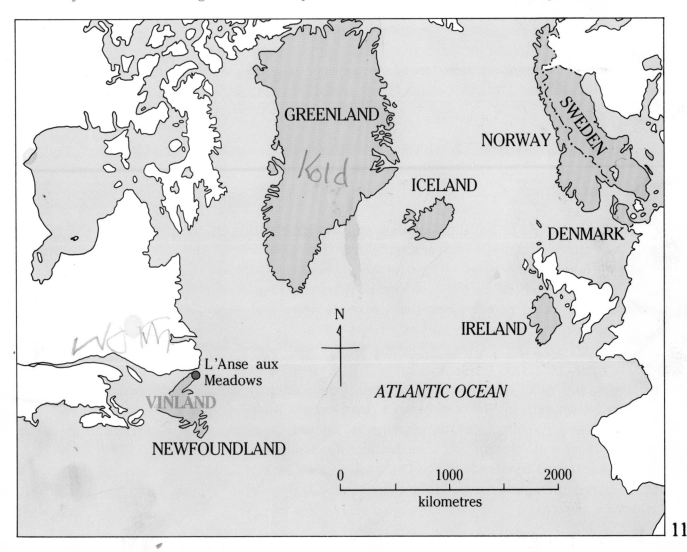

The Vikings Move to Vinland

The Vikings built two houses and stayed in Vinland for the winter. They cut down trees so that they could use the wood to build ships. When summer came, the Vikings loaded their knorr with wood and sailed back to Greenland.

The Vikings in Greenland were excited when they heard about the wonderful new place called Vinland. A few years later a group of Vikings decided to move to Vinland. They took cattle and sheep with them.

One of the women who went to live in Vinland was called Gudrun. While she was in Vinland, Gudrun gave birth to a baby boy. She named him Snorri. Snorri was the first European born in Canada.

One day some Indians visited the Viking settlement. They traded furs for milk and cloth. Later the Vikings and the Indians began to quarrel. There were several battles. At last the Vikings decided to go back to Greenland. After living in the wide meadows of Vinland for three years, the Vikings packed up all their belongings and sailed away. As the years passed other Vikings visited Vinland, but no one stayed there very long.

How do you suppose the Indians felt when the Vikings came to live in their land? Why do you think the Vikings and the Indians began to quarrel?

The Vikings loved to tell their families and friends about their adventures. Hundreds of years ago these stories were collected and written down. The stories are called the *Icelandic Sagas*. Two **sagas** tell how Vinland was found and settled. After a while, people forgot that the sagas told a true story. They forgot that Vinland really existed.

No one knows exactly where Vinland was. It could have been in many places on the east **coast** of North America. In the 1960s, the ruins of a Viking settlement were found in northern Newfoundland. The ruins are at a place called L'Anse aux Meadows. They include the remains of houses, boat sheds, a blacksmith's shop and two fire pits. Many people believe that L'Anse aux Meadows was Leif the Lucky's Vinland. If that is true, then people from Europe were living in Canada 1000 years ago.

Leif the Lucky discovers Vinland with some other Vikings. What might the Vikings do next?

Explorers from Europe Cross the Atlantic

After the Vikings left Vinland, hundreds of years passed. The *Icelandic Sagas* were forgotten. People in Europe did not know about the land across the Atlantic Ocean.

Then **merchants** in Europe began looking for a new **route** to China. They wanted to get silks, spices and jewels from China to sell to people in Europe. For a long time the merchants had sent camel caravans eastward across Asia to China. That route was long and dangerous. The merchants wanted to find an easier, safer route.

By this time, many sailors knew the earth was round. They said that if a ship sailed west across the Atlantic Ocean, it would come to China. Some merchants in Europe decided to send ships across the Atlantic Ocean to find out if this was true.

The people who set out in ships to cross the ocean were explorers. They were going where other Europeans had not been before. They were going into the unknown. To do that, they had to be brave and adventurous.

How do you think the explorers felt when they set out across the Atlantic Ocean? Would you like to have been one of those first explorers? Why or why not?

What Were the Explorers Looking For?

The explorers wanted to find a sea route to China. Soon they discovered that the **continent** of North America lay between the Atlantic Ocean and China. When the explorers first saw North America, they thought they had reached India. They called the people they met there "Indians." Later the explorers began to look for a passage around North America. The explorers thought this passage would take them north and west. For this reason they called it the **Northwest Passage**.

Most of the explorers who came to Canada from Europe were looking for the Northwest Passage. Some were looking for other things as well. Many wanted to get furs. Others were looking for gold, silver or copper. All the explorers wanted to find out more about Canada.

What do you think was the most important reason that explorers came to Canada?

Long ago, merchants and explorers sailed in ships like this one. Would you like to cross the ocean in this ship?

How Did the Indians Help the Explorers?

The explorers could not have gone very far without help from the Indians. The Indians had lived in Canada for thousands of years. They knew how to travel through the thick forests and across the wide prairies. The Indians knew which rivers to take and how to get around dangerous **rapids** and waterfalls. They acted as **guides** for the explorers.

The Indians also taught the explorers how to survive in the wilderness. The explorers learned how to make and use canoes and snowshoes. While they were exploring, they wore practical Indian clothing, such as moccasins and warm fur suits. The Indians also taught the explorers how to hunt for and prepare food.

What might have happened to the explorers if the Indians had not helped them?

This map shows the northern part of the earth. Can you see why it took so long for people in Europe to find a route to China?

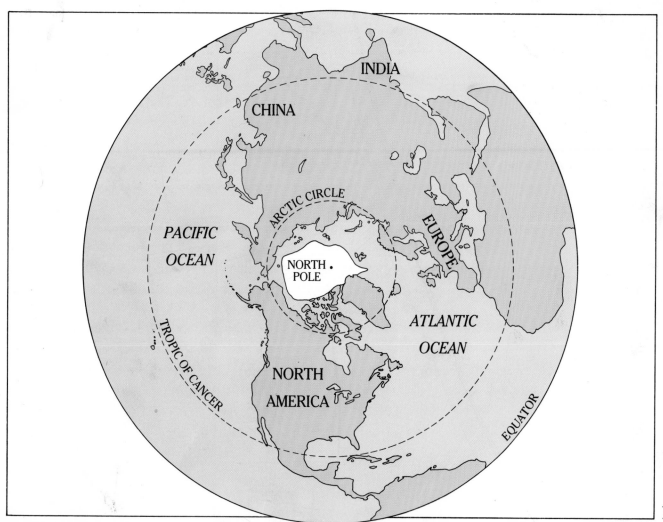

What Did the Explorers Find Out about Canada?

As they searched for the Northwest Passage, the explorers from Europe learned about the **geography** of our country. They **charted** the bays, rivers, lakes and mountains. This means that they made notes and drew maps of these features. The explorers also learned about the plants, animals and birds that lived in the forests and on the prairies.

The eastern part of Canada was the first **region** to be explored. Then some of the explorers journeyed across the prairies. Other explorers went north to the Arctic. Later some of the explorers charted the Pacific Coast. Others went through the western mountains to the Pacific Ocean. As the explorers moved across the country, they learned about its many different regions. Each explorer added a new region to the map of Canada.

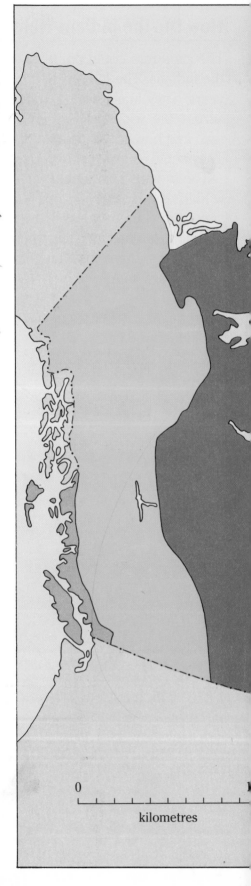

The explorers learned about Canada's geographical regions. Which region do you live in?

0   k

kilometres

16

The Five Major Explorers in This Book

Many explorers came to Canada. The rest of this book tells mainly about five of those explorers. Each one explored a different region of Canada. Here are the five explorers and the regions they explored:

Samuel de Champlain   Eastern Canada
Anthony Henday   The Prairies
Samuel Hearne   The Barren Grounds
George Vancouver   The Pacific Coast
Alexander Mackenzie   The Western Mountains

In the chapters ahead, you will discover what each of the five explorers was looking for. You will also find out how the Indians helped each explorer. Finally, you will learn what each explorer discovered about the geography of the vast new country, Canada.

Who thought of Canada as a new country? Was it new to the Indians?

The story of the explorers is an exciting part of our country's history. Imagine what it must be like to go into the unknown. Imagine paddling your canoe in rivers filled with rapids. Imagine climbing mountains that seem to go on forever. As you read this book, you will share in the excitement of exploring. You will find out what it meant to be one of Canada's first explorers.

Champlain explored eastern Canada. This picture shows the rocky Atlantic coast.

Henday explored the prairies. He saw flat land covered with grass.

Hearne went across the Barren Grounds. He saw flowers and small plants but no trees.

Vancouver mapped the Pacific Coast. He saw high mountains and vast forests.

Mackenzie crossed the western mountains. He paddled along many rivers on his journey.

2

Who Explored Eastern Canada?

Cabot and Cartier Lead the Way

What Lies Ahead?

In the first part of this chapter, you will find out the answers to these questions.

- Who was John Cabot?

- What was Cabot looking for?

- Who was Jacques Cartier?

- What was Cartier looking for?

- What did Cabot and Cartier find out about eastern Canada?

Cabot was a trader and mapmaker. Why would he be a good person to look for a new route to China?

Cabot Tries to Reach China

About 500 years ago, explorers from Europe began to cross the Atlantic Ocean. They were looking for a new route to China. They did not know that North America lay between the Atlantic Ocean and China.

One of the explorers who dreamed of finding a route to China was John Cabot. He was a trader and mapmaker from Italy. Cabot went to England. He told merchants there of his plan to reach China by going west across the Atlantic Ocean. The merchants thought that was a good idea. They gave him enough money to buy a small ship. Cabot named it the *Matthew*. It carried 18 men.

Why would merchants want Cabot to find a route to China?

In May 1497, the *Matthew* sailed from England. After 54 days at sea, Cabot sighted land. No one knows for sure where Cabot landed. He probably landed in present-day Newfoundland or Cape Breton Island.

Cabot thought he had reached China. He raised the English flag and **claimed** the country for the king of England. Then Cabot sailed along the coast looking for cities where he could buy silks, spices and jewels. Instead, he saw endless forests. Although Cabot saw traps set for animals and axe marks on the trees, he did not meet any people.

At last Cabot decided to go back to England. On the way he sailed south of Newfoundland. He found that the ocean there was filled with fish. When Cabot dipped a basket into the water, it came up loaded with cod. This fishing area is now called the Grand Banks. When fishermen in Europe heard about the Grand Banks, they began sailing across the ocean to fish there.

Cabot found the Grand Banks when he was exploring eastern Canada. What can you tell about the Grand Banks from this map?

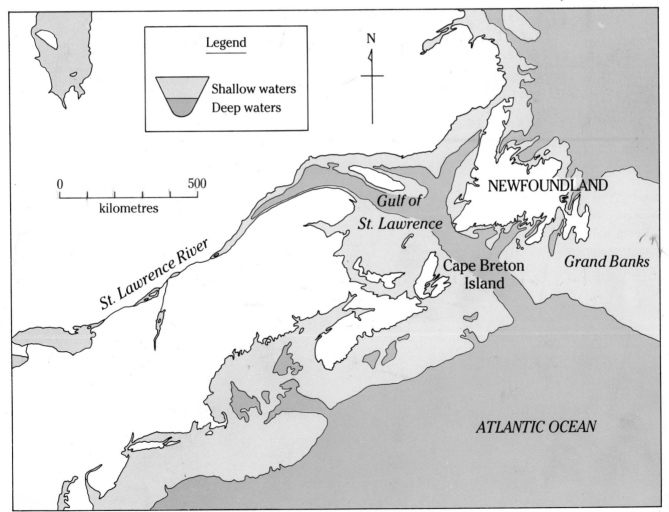

Cabot prepares to leave on his second voyage across the Atlantic Ocean. Who are some of the people seeing him off? What might they be saying to him?

Cabot decided to make a second voyage. In 1498 he sailed from England with five ships. No one knows what happened after that. Some people think that Cabot explored the eastern coast of North America before he returned to England.

John Cabot never reached China. He did discover one of the best fishing grounds in the world.

The Beginning of the Fur Trade

Fishing boats from Europe sailed across the Atlantic Ocean to the Grand Banks. Sometimes the fishermen went ashore to dry their fish or mend their nets. There they met the Indians. Often the fishermen would trade iron or clothing for furs from the Indians.

People in Europe liked the furs the fishermen brought back. The fishermen found they could get a lot of money for the furs. Soon merchants from Europe began sailing across the Atlantic Ocean. They, too, wanted to trade goods for furs from the Indians. This was the beginning of the **fur trade**.

Cartier Searches for the Northwest Passage

After a while people realized that Cabot had not reached China. Instead, he had found a large land mass between Europe and China. People still wanted to find a route to China. Explorers began to look for a passage around the new land. It was called the Northwest Passage. One of these explorers was a Frenchman named Jacques Cartier.

In 1534 Cartier left France with two ships. The ships sailed across the Atlantic Ocean. They went around the northern tip of Newfoundland. Then they sailed into what is now called the Gulf of St. Lawrence.

Cartier and his men spent the summer exploring the **gulf**. There they met some Indians who offered them seal meat and furs. Cartier was happy to take some furs back to Europe. He knew the people there would like them.

Cartier explored all the bays in the Gulf of St. Lawrence. At the entrance to one of the bays, he raised a cross and shield. He claimed the land for the king of France.

Was it fair to the Indians that Cartier claimed the land for France?

Why Did People in Europe Want Furs?

In Europe, men liked to wear fur hats. Sometimes the hats were decorated with a few small feathers or flowers. Men were proud of their fur hats and took special care of them.

The most common type of fur used for these hats was beaver. Beaver fur from Canada was even thicker and more beautiful than beaver fur from Europe. For this reason furs from Canada were in great demand.

How Did Canada Get Its Name?

Cartier called the new land Canada, but no one knows for sure how our country got its name. Some people think Canada comes from the Indian word *kanata*, which means "village" or "dwellings." Perhaps Cartier heard some Indians call a village *kanata*. Perhaps he thought they meant the whole country. Other people think that Canada might come from another Indian word, *kan-atak*, which means "sacred place."

According to another story, some people from Spain were looking for gold in Canada. When they didn't find any, they said, *"Aca nada."* That means "Here is nothing" in Spanish.

The Indians show Cartier how to cure scurvy. What is the Indian putting into the pot?

The next year Cartier went back to the Gulf of St. Lawrence and sailed into the St. Lawrence River. He and his men went up the river to an Indian village called Hochelaga. Cartier did not go any farther because the river was filled with rapids. He and his men went back to an Indian village called Stadacona. They spent the winter there. The weather was very cold. Many of the men became ill with **scurvy**. Their legs became swollen. Their gums rotted and their teeth fell out. Some of the men died.

The Indians knew a cure for scurvy. They taught Cartier how to make tea from the leaves and bark of a white cedar tree. After the sick men drank the tea, they got better. Now we know that scurvy is caused by lack of vitamin C. The leaves and bark of the white cedar tree are rich in vitamin C.

How do you think the Indians knew about a cure for scurvy?

When spring came, Cartier and his men sailed back to France. Cartier had not found the Northwest Passage. Instead, he had explored and charted the Gulf of St. Lawrence and the St. Lawrence River. This river could take ships hundreds of kilometres into Canada.

What Have We Learned?

John Cabot was looking for a new route to China. Instead, he landed in Canada, probably in Newfoundland or on Cape Breton Island. Cabot also discovered the great fishing grounds called the Grand Banks.

Jacques Cartier came to Canada to find the Northwest Passage. Instead, he discovered the Gulf of St. Lawrence and the St. Lawrence River. He also traded with the Indians for furs.

This map shows the routes of Cartier's journeys. No one knows Cabot's route. How is this fact shown on the map?

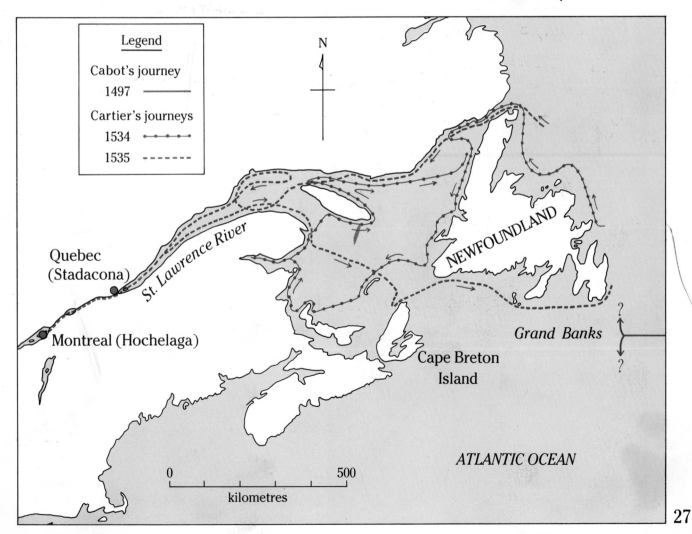

Legend

Cabot's journey
1497

Cartier's journeys
1534
1535

N

Quebec (Stadacona)

Montreal (Hochelaga)

St. Lawrence River

NEWFOUNDLAND

Grand Banks

Cape Breton Island

ATLANTIC OCEAN

0   500
kilometres

The Appalachian Region

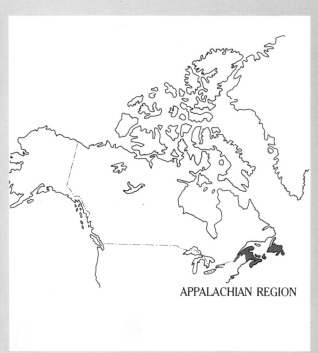

APPALACHIAN REGION

The part of Canada that Cabot and Cartier explored is called the Appalachian region. It is located next to the Atlantic Ocean. The pictures show what this region looks like today.

The region includes a long **range** of mountains called the Appalachians. The mountains are very old. Over the years they have been worn down. Today they are low and rounded.

When Cabot and Cartier sailed along the coast, they saw huge forests. Most trees were **coniferous**. The branches of these evergreen trees are never bare. Cartier thought the whole Appalachian region must be covered

Left: This is a farm in the Appalachian Mountains. You can see how low and rounded the mountains are.

Right: These farmers are harvesting potatoes.

with trees. In fact, this region also includes rocky places and many lakes and ponds.

Imagine sailing along the Atlantic coast today. It looks quite different from the way it looked when Cabot and Cartier were there. Most of the forests along the shore are gone. For many years people cut down trees to use for the masts of sailing ships and for lumber. Later, settlers cleared forests for farming. Today most farming takes place along the coast and in the river valleys. The soil is good there. Many farmers grow potatoes or apples.

You will also see cities and fishing villages along the coast. Many people here fish or work in fish plants. Cabot had made an important discovery when he found the Grand Banks.

There are still large forests farther inland. Much of the soil in the Appalachian region is poor for growing anything but trees. Some trees are sold as Christmas trees. Many are used for lumber and for making paper. Many people work in sawmills and paper mills.

Left: The Appalachian region has many forests and lakes. Most trees are coniferous.

Left: Many people work in fish plants.

Right: Many towns are near sawmills.

29

Samuel de Champlain Comes to Canada

What Lies Ahead?

In this part of the chapter, you will find out the answers to these questions.

- Who was Samuel de Champlain?

- What was Champlain looking for?

- How did the Indians help Champlain?

- What new things did Champlain find out about Canada?

Many years had passed since John Cabot and Jacques Cartier had come to Canada. Fishermen were crossing the Atlantic Ocean to fish for cod on the Grand Banks. Traders were sailing into the Gulf of St. Lawrence to trade with the Indians for furs. Explorers were still looking for the Northwest Passage.

In 1603 Samuel de Champlain came to Canada from France. He came with some people who wanted to set up a **colony** and live in Canada. Then it would be easier for them to explore the country and to look for the Northwest Passage. It would also be easier to get furs.

How would starting a colony make it easier to explore Canada?

Champlain Explores Acadia and Builds Port Royal

On Champlain's first voyage to Canada, his job was to draw maps and make a report on the country. When he got back to France, he told the king that Canada was a fine land.

The next year Champlain went back to Canada and explored Acadia. Today that part of Canada is called Nova Scotia and New Brunswick. Champlain and his men built a fort on an island at the **mouth** of the St. Croix River. They spent the winter there. The winter was harsh, and the island was exposed to the winds. Great **ice floes** filled the river. The explorers could not cross the river to hunt for food or to cut firewood on the **mainland**. They had to eat cold salt meat and cold, uncooked vegetables. Even the cider froze and each man was given his cider in a hunk. Many men died of scurvy.

The next year the settlement was moved across the Bay of Fundy to Port Royal. There the colony was protected from the wind. The forest supplied plenty of wood all year round. Champlain and his men planted a vegetable garden at Port Royal. They also dug a stream and put some trout in it. Now they would always have fresh food.

Who Was Samuel de Champlain?

Champlain was born in 1567 in a small seaport on the Atlantic coast of France. As a young man he served in the French army. Later Champlain visited other countries and wrote a book about his journeys. In 1603 he crossed the Atlantic Ocean to Canada. This was the first of Champlain's many voyages to Canada. Later he wrote a book about his explorations in Canada, and that is how we know what happened.

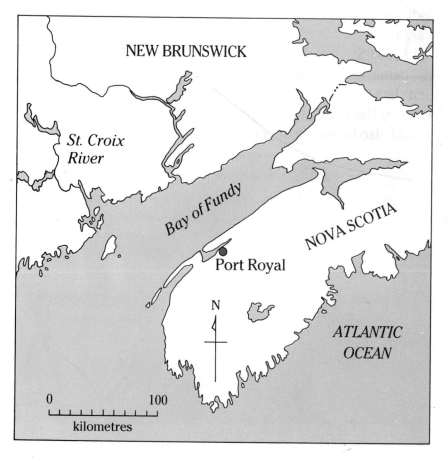

Champlain built a fort on an island at the mouth of the St. Croix River. The next year he moved to Port Royal. What body of water separates these two places?

31

In 1606 the explorers spent a second winter at Port Royal. To keep the men in good spirits, Champlain started the Order of Good Cheer. Each man had to provide food for one day. It included a special treat, like beaver tails or salmon. When dinner time came, the host would march in with a napkin over his shoulder. The other men marched in behind him, each carrying a dish. At the end of the meal, the men raised their glasses and wished each other good health. Some of the men also put on plays. In this way, everybody at Port Royal had something to do during the long winter.

Why was the colony at Port Royal more successful than the colony on the island?

Members of the Order of Good Cheer march in with the dinner. Why was the Order of Good Cheer a good idea?

Champlain Moves to Quebec

In 1608 Champlain moved from Port Royal to the **site** of the old Indian village Stadacona. He built a fort at the place where the St. Lawrence River narrows. The Indians called this place *kebec*, which means "narrows." Champlain called it Quebec.

At Quebec, Champlain made friends with the Montagnais, Algonquin and Huron Indians. Champlain needed their help to go exploring and to get furs.

That same year a youth named Étienne Brûlé came to Quebec from France. Champlain later sent Brûlé to live with the Indians and learn their language. That way Brûlé could be Champlain's **interpreter** when they were exploring.

What was Brûlé's special job? Why was it important?

Journey to the Land of the Iroquois

In the spring of 1609, the Montagnais, Algonquins and Hurons went to fight the Iroquois Indians. Champlain went along to help his friends.

We don't know for sure if Brûlé went on the journey to the land of the Iroquois. It is possible that he did go. Let's imagine that he went with Champlain and that he wrote this story.

Étienne Brûlé's Story

After six days of feasting and dancing, we set out from Quebec. The Indians were in their birch-bark canoes. We followed them, rowing our shallop. Our heavy boat was no match for the light Indian canoes. The Indians left us far behind. We did not see them again until we reached the River of the Iroquois. The Indians were camped on the shore waiting for us.

At first the River of the Iroquois was easy going. It was bordered with thick woods. We saw many oak trees, nut trees and vines. The river was filled with fish.

Who Was Étienne Brûlé?

Not much is known about Étienne Brûlé. We do know that he was born around 1592 in a small town south of Paris, France. Brûlé was only 16 when he came to Quebec in 1608. We also know that Brûlé loved adventure. Later he lived with the Indians for many years. He learned to hunt and to paddle a birch-bark canoe as well as they could.

33

Then we came to some rapids. The Indians said we would have to make a **portage**. We watched them pick up their canoes as if they were feathers and carry them around the rapids. I looked at Champlain and knew what he was thinking. Our shallop was too heavy. How could we pick it up and carry it around rapids? Champlain decided that from now on he would use an Indian canoe.

I was happy to escape from our shallop into a canoe. Now we could explore any river we liked without worrying about how to get around rapids.

At last we came to a lake. In the lake there were many beautiful islands covered with woods and meadows. There were animals and birds everywhere on the islands. Champlain named the lake after himself—Lake Champlain.

Champlain and Brûlé watch the Indians pick up their canoes to carry them around the rapids. What might Champlain be saying to Brûlé?

We paddled along the lake until we came to the Iroquois camp. A battle was fought. I had never been in a battle before, so I wasn't sure what to do. Champlain posted me in the woods. He told me to fire my arquebus when I heard him shoot. I don't think I hit anybody, but the arquebus made a loud bang. Our Indian friends said the noise helped them win. Afterwards, we had a victory feast and dance.

I enjoyed exploring most of all. After that I liked feasting and dancing. I decided I could get along without fighting battles. Perhaps the Indians felt that way, too.

How was a canoe better suited for exploring Canada than a shallop?

Right: In 1609 Champlain travelled along the River of the Iroquois to Lake Champlain. What is the River of the Iroquois called today?

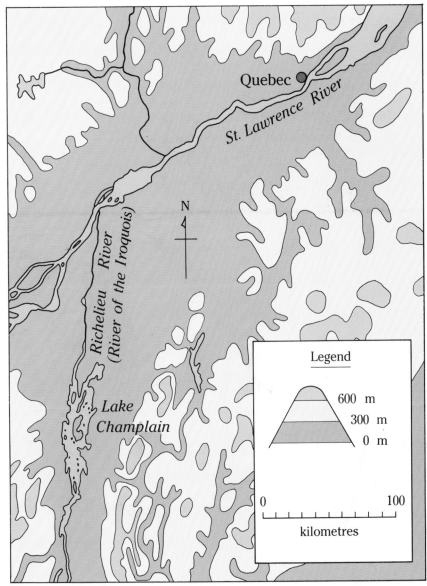

Quebec

St. Lawrence River

N

Richelieu River
(River of the Iroquois)

Lake Champlain

Legend

600 m

300 m

0 m

0   100

kilometres

How the Indians Built Birch-Bark Canoes

The Indians who were with Champlain travelled in birch-bark canoes. Champlain decided to use a birch-bark canoe instead of a shallop. The birch-bark canoe was lighter than the shallop. It was easier to carry on long portages around rapids or waterfalls.

The canoe was made from birch bark and cedar branches. Spruce roots were used to sew the canoe together. Spruce gum was used for sealing the seams. Because all these materials came from trees, a canoe could be made or repaired wherever there were trees.

It took about 10 days to build a birch-bark canoe. A good canoe could last 20 years.

These are the tools the Indians used to build the canoe.

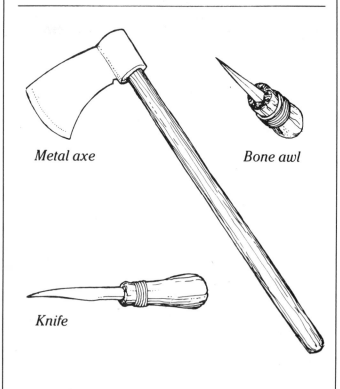

Metal axe

Bone awl

Knife

This is how the Indians built canoes.

1. *The first step was to make a cut in a birch tree with an axe. Then the bark was peeled off.*

2. *Sometimes a single sheet of bark was used for the canoe. Other times several sheets of bark were sewn together with spruce roots. A bone awl was used to make holes in the bark. The spruce roots were then pulled through the holes.*

3. Next the bark was laid on the ground. A frame made of cedar was placed on top of it. Rocks were put on top of the frame to hold it in place.

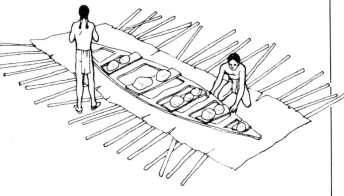

4. Stakes were driven into the bark beside the frame. Pairs of stakes on opposite sides of the frame were tied together. The bark was pulled up and lashed to the stakes.

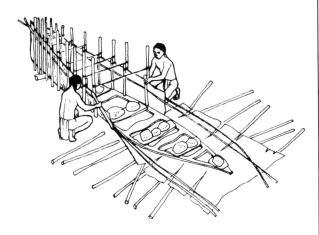

5. Next the rocks were removed. The frame was raised to its proper height. Then the bark was sewn to the frame with spruce roots. Some spruce gum was heated and mixed with animal fat. The mixture was smeared over the seams to keep out water.

6. Finally, strips of cedar were put into the bottom of the canoe. Then a knife was used to carve ribs from the trunk of a cedar. The ribs were placed over the cedar strips. Now the canoe was complete.

Search for the Northern Ocean

In 1610, Champlain sent Brûlé to live with the Algonquins. Champlain wanted Brûlé to learn their language and to see what the country was like. As far as we know, Brûlé lived with the Indians for the next four years.

Champlain also sent a young Frenchman named Nicolas de Vignau to live with some other Algonquins. They lived beside the Ottawa River. When Vignau saw Champlain again, he told Champlain that he had made a journey to a great ocean in the north. This was exciting news for Champlain. He thought this ocean might lead to the Northwest Passage. In 1613 Champlain and Vignau set out with some Algonquin guides up the Ottawa River. They were searching for the Northern Ocean. Let us pretend that Champlain told Brûlé about his journey with Vignau. Imagine that Brûlé wrote down the story.

Étienne Brûlé's Story

Champlain told me about the day he almost lost his life. He was walking on the shore, dragging his canoe through a rapid. The line was tied around his wrist. The water was so swift that it sounded like thunder as it crashed over the rocks. Suddenly the canoe turned over into a whirlpool. Champlain fell to the ground and was pulled between two rocks. The line to his canoe tightened around his wrist, nearly cutting his hand off. Champlain cried for help and began pulling the canoe towards him. One of the Indians ran to his aid, but by then Champlain had pulled the canoe out of the whirlpool. Although he was out of danger, there was a deep cut in his wrist. After that, Champlain and the Indians decided to rest for a day.

How might Champlain have avoided cutting his wrist? What could he have done differently?

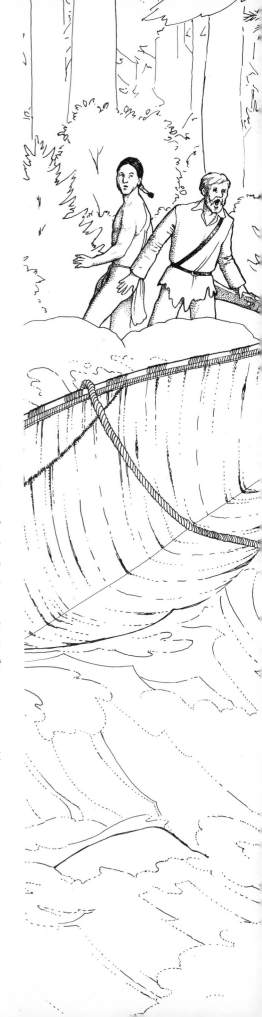

Champlain has fallen between two rocks. What might have happened if he had fallen into the whirlpool?

The day came when the explorers left the Ottawa River. They began a long portage through bogs and across shallow lakes. Anything that could not be easily carried was left behind. The explorers did not even take food with them. They lived on berries and fish they caught in the lakes. Then at last Champlain and his men reached Allumette Lake. They came to a large Algonquin village.

Étienne Brûlé's Story

Champlain told me that the Algonquins in the village gave a big feast for him. When the feast was over, Champlain told the chief that he wanted to go to the Northern Ocean. Champlain said that Vignau had already been there. The chief said that Vignau had not. The chief said that Vignau was not telling the truth.

Champlain did not know what to do. Vignau said he was telling the truth. The Indians insisted that he was not. The Indians said they had lived in this place all their lives but had never been to the Northern Ocean. They did not even know the way. How, then, could Vignau possibly know how to get there?

Champlain took Vignau aside and told him that he must tell the truth. At last Vignau admitted that he had told Champlain a lie. He fell on his knees and begged Champlain to forgive him.

Champlàin was so angry he could not speak. He went off by himself until he had calmed down.

I don't blame Champlain for being angry. But I'm not sure that Vignau was lying. Maybe he really had gone to the Northern Ocean.

Anyway, that was the end of the journey to the Northern Ocean. I know that Champlain was disappointed. He wanted to find the Northwest Passage. Now he had to make the long journey back to Quebec.

Do you think that Vignau was telling the truth? Why or why not? Do we have any way of knowing for sure?

Journey to the Land of the Hurons

When Champlain got back to Quebec, he made plans for another journey. The Hurons had told him of great waters to the west. Champlain thought these waters might be the Western Ocean. He hoped to sail across the Western Ocean to China.

In 1615, Champlain set out on his last and greatest journey. Étienne Brûlé was with him.

Étienne Brûlé's Story

Have you ever been so excited about going on a journey that you can hardly wait to start? That was how I felt before we began our journey up the Ottawa River. I lay awake all night waiting for the sun to rise, waiting to be on the river in my canoe. I could see from the way Champlain talked and smiled that he was happy to be off exploring again, too.

On his journey with Vignau, Champlain visited some Indians at Allumette Lake. Can you find this lake on the map?

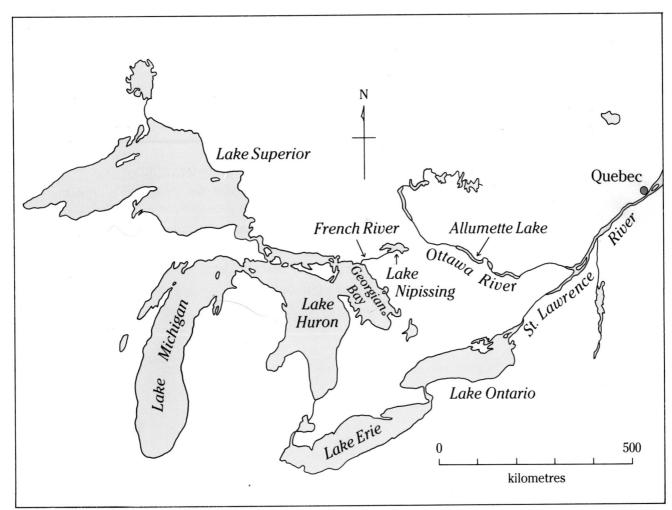

41

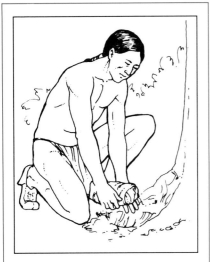

What Was Sagamité?

When travelling, the Indians often buried dried corn in birch-bark packages. Then, when they needed food, they dug up the corn they had buried earlier. The corn was placed on a skin and pounded with flat stones. Then it was boiled in a container of hot water. If there was any meat or fish, it was added to the mush. Going up the Ottawa River, the Indians and the explorers often had this dish for their supper. It was called **sagamité**.

We left on July 9. There were many rapids along the river. We had to make long and difficult portages. The rocks bruised our feet. The brambles cut our legs. The mosquitoes were terrible. I didn't mind, though, and neither did Champlain.

After a while the river narrowed. Large fish leaped from the water. We saw many herons and loons. Wild raspberries and blueberries grew in open places by the river. As we made portages, we gathered berries by the handful. There were days when berries were all we had to eat. We didn't have time to fish or hunt for deer.

At last the explorers arrived at Lake Nipissing. The Algonquins who lived there were pleased to see Champlain. They gave feasts in his honour. After spending two days with the Algonquins, the explorers left the lake and entered the French River.

Étienne Brûlé's Story

*The land along the river was wild and **barren**. We saw nothing but bare rocks and mountains. On the way down the river, we met some Indians. They had come to the river to gather and dry blueberries to use as food in the winter. The Indians dry berries just as people in France dry plums. Champlain gave the chief a hatchet. The chief took a piece of charcoal and drew a picture of his country on a sheet of bark.*

*The next day we came to a great body of water. The first thing Champlain did was dip his hand into the water and taste it. He hoped the water would be salty, but it was **fresh**. Then he knew he had not reached the Western Ocean. Champlain named these waters the Sweet Sea.*

How do you think Champlain felt when he realized that he had not reached the Western Ocean?

Champlain had reached the part of Lake Huron that is called Georgian Bay today. Champlain now turned south towards the land of the Hurons. It was a rich land filled with tall maple, oak, beech and elm trees. There were many streams where the Hurons could catch fish.

Champlain visited several Huron villages. The Hurons had cleared the land so that they could grow corn, beans and squash. At one village the Hurons gave Champlain a feast of bread, squash and fish. At last Champlain arrived at the main village.

The chief is drawing a map on a piece of bark. How might this map help Champlain?

The St. Lawrence Lowland

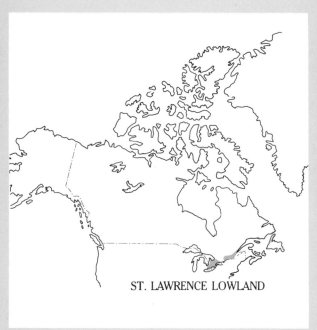

ST. LAWRENCE LOWLAND

The St. Lawrence Lowland is a small region in eastern Canada. It is the land along the St. Lawrence River and near the Great Lakes. Champlain explored part of this region with the Hurons. The pictures show you what it looks like today.

Long ago the St. Lawrence Lowland was covered by a large sea. Today this land is flat or gently rolling. In some places there are marshes where flocks of sea birds gather.

When Champlain explored the St. Lawrence Lowland, it was covered with forests. He saw

Left: The St. Lawrence Lowland has many deciduous trees. The leaves turn beautiful colours in autumn.

Right: These farmers are planting tomatoes.

many types of coniferous trees. He also saw many **deciduous** trees. In autumn, the leaves of these trees change colour and fall off. Champlain would have seen their beautiful red, yellow and orange leaves. The forest floors were carpeted with ferns and tiny wildflowers.

Imagine travelling down the St. Lawrence River and through the Great Lakes today. Almost everything has changed. Most of the forests have been cleared for farmland. The flat land and **fertile** soil are good for farming. Many farmers grow vegetables, fruit or tobacco. They also grow food for animals. Other farmers have dairy cows, beef cattle or chickens.

The St. Lawrence Lowland was one of the first areas settled by Europeans. They started farms and built cities. More and more settlers came. Some started factories. Today many things are made here, such as clothing, food and cars. Many people live and work in this region, even though it is only a small part of Canada.

Above: You can see marshes in places along the St. Lawrence River.

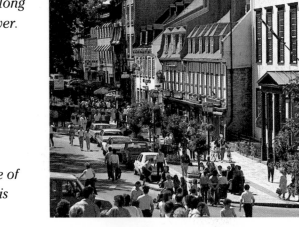

Right: Quebec is one of the many cities in this region.

45

Champlain and Brûlé say goodbye as Brûlé prepares to leave with the Huron Indians. How might Brûlé be feeling?

Étienne Brûlé's Story

The Hurons at the main village were very happy to see Champlain. They held feasts and dances to welcome him. Then they asked Champlain to help them fight the Iroquois. Champlain said he would.

The Hurons decided to send messengers to other Indians asking them to help fight the Iroquois. I asked Champlain if I could go with the messengers. I told him I might be able to find a passage to the Western Ocean. Champlain decided it would be a good idea for me to go.

I was sorry to leave Champlain. I liked exploring with him. He was a brave man and a good leader. When something went wrong, he didn't get upset. He understood the Indians, and they understood him.

I said goodbye to Champlain. Then I set out with the Huron messengers.

What makes a person a good leader on a journey?

What Happened to Étienne Brûlé?

After Brûlé and the Huron messengers left Champlain, Brûlé explored far to the south. Then he returned to the land of the Hurons. He saw Champlain once again in 1618.

Brûlé lived with the Hurons for the rest of his life. He liked the free life in the forests. He was happy paddling on the rivers, hunting and fishing with the Indians. Brûlé dressed like an Indian. He knew the Huron language as well as he knew French.

While Brûlé was living with the Hurons, he explored much of the Great Lakes region. He was probably the first European to see all five of the Great Lakes.

In 1633 Brûlé was killed by the Hurons. We don't know why they killed him. We do know that Brûlé did much to help Champlain explore Canada.

What Happened to Samuel de Champlain?

After Champlain left Brûlé in 1615, he crossed Lake Ontario with the Huron warriors. When they got to the Iroquois country a battle was fought. Champlain and the Hurons were defeated by the Iroquois. Champlain was wounded in the battle.

Champlain went to live with the Hurons for the winter. While he was staying in their country, he saw how the Hurons lived. He admired their way of life.

At last spring came. Champlain said goodbye to the Hurons and travelled back to Quebec.

Champlain did not do any more exploring in Canada. Instead, he built up the colony at Quebec. More and more settlers arrived from France. Champlain's dream of building a new country was coming true.

Champlain died at Quebec on Christmas Day in 1635. Today he is remembered as the Father of Canada.

What Have We Learned?

John Cabot and Jacques Cartier were the first explorers in eastern Canada. Both Cabot and Cartier wanted to find a route to China. Instead, Cabot found the Grand Banks fishing area. Cartier discovered the Gulf of St. Lawrence and the St. Lawrence River.

Later Samuel de Champlain came to Canada. He, too, wanted to find the Northwest Passage. He also wanted to build a colony and help start the fur trade.

Many Indians helped Champlain. They knew what rivers and paths to take. They also taught him that a birch-bark canoe was best for exploring the rivers and lakes of Canada.

Champlain did not find the Northwest Passage. He did not find any passage to the Western Ocean. He did find out a lot about the geography of eastern Canada. He explored Acadia and the St. Lawrence region. He also built a colony at Quebec. The colony was a base for getting furs and for exploring.

In this chapter we have learned about some of the people who explored eastern Canada from 1497 to 1635. Can you find that time period on the line below?

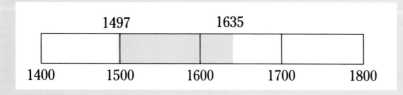

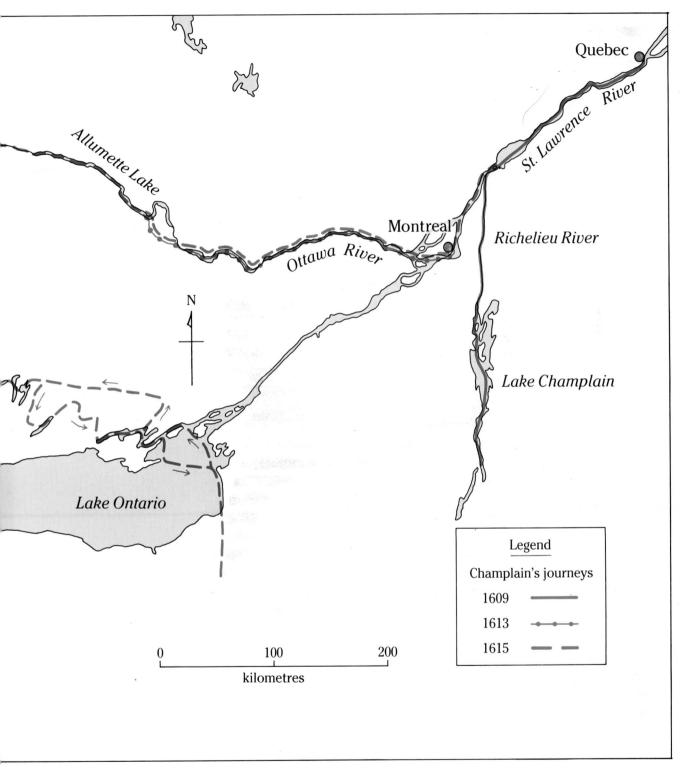

Quebec

St. Lawrence River

Allumette Lake

Montreal

Richelieu River

Ottawa River

N

Lake Champlain

Lake Ontario

Legend

Champlain's journeys

1609 ————

1613 •—•—•

1615 – – –

0   100   200

kilometres

In this chapter you have learned about three of Champlain's journeys. This map shows the routes of those journeys. On which journey did Champlain travel farthest west?

Two Points of View

The Europeans who came to Canada in the 1600s did different things. At first, most of the people were explorers or fur traders. Then settlers began to arrive. They wanted to live in the new colony at Quebec. They wanted to start farms there.

Étienne Brûlé and Madame Hébert are two of the people who helped our country in its early years. Let's hear what they have to say about what they did.

Étienne Brûlé

The outdoor life is for me. I enjoy fishing and hunting with my Indian friends. I like paddling my canoe and seeing new places. I feel good when I'm travelling along the beautiful rivers and through the forests in this new country. I am happiest when I am exploring. I hope that some day I'll find the Western Ocean.

What things were important to Brûlé?
Why were people like Brûlé needed in Canada's early years?

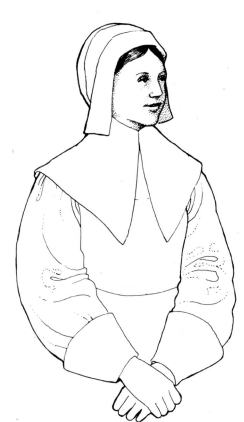

Madame Hébert

My family lives in the new settlement at Quebec. We are building a colony in the Canadian wilderness. Right now our settlement is very small, but new families arrive every year. Many of the colonists are starting farms here. We are all working hard. We clear the land, plant crops and build houses and barns. My family enjoys being part of this new community.

What things were important to Madame Hébert?
Why were people like Madame Hébert needed in Canada's early years?

Looking Back

Explorers and Their Achievements

Match the explorers in the first list with the achievements in the second list.

Explorers

a. Jacques Cartier
b. Étienne Brûlé
c. John Cabot
d. Samuel de Champlain

Achievements

1. I learned the Algonquin language and worked as Champlain's interpreter.
2. I discovered the Grand Banks fishing area.
3. I started colonies in Acadia and at Quebec.
4. I explored the Gulf of St. Lawrence and the St. Lawrence River.
5. I tried to find the Western Ocean. Instead I discovered the Sweet Sea.

How the Indians Helped

Champlain found that a birch-bark canoe was better for travelling in Canada than a shallop. Find the picture in this chapter that shows both a canoe and a shallop. What can you tell about the canoe from the picture? Write a paragraph about what might have happened if Champlain had not used a canoe.

Geography of Eastern Canada

Cabot and Cartier explored the Appalachian region of eastern Canada. Champlain explored the Appalachian region and the St. Lawrence Lowland. Look back at the special pages about these two regions. Make a list of the things the explorers would have seen in the Appalachian region. Then make a list of the things you would see there today. Now make the same two lists for the St. Lawrence Lowland. What has changed the most in each region?

Imagine You Were There

What would you have said or done —
  if you were an Algonquin Indian in eastern Canada when fishermen and fur traders began to arrive from Europe?
  if Champlain had asked you to move to Acadia and help build a colony?
  if you had been with Champlain when he reached the Sweet Sea?

Find Out More

1. The explorers who travelled through eastern Canada met Iroquois, Algonquin, Huron and Montagnais Indians. Pick one of these Indian groups. Use your library to find out what kind of homes those Indians used to build. Draw a picture of one of those homes.
2. Go to the library and find out more about Champlain. Write a paragraph about the new things you have learned.
3. Find out more about the marshes in the St. Lawrence Lowland. See if you can find pictures of some of the different kinds of sea birds that live there.

3

Who Explored the Prairies?

Kelsey and the La Vérendryes Lead the Way

What Lies Ahead?

In the first part of this chapter, you will find out the answers to these questions.

- Who was Henry Kelsey?

- Where did Kelsey go and what did he see?

- Who were the La Vérendryes?

- Where did the La Vérendryes go and what did they see?

- What did Kelsey and the La Vérendryes find out about the prairies?

Champlain had explored and mapped eastern Canada with the help of the Indians. They had not found the Northwest Passage.

Other explorers were also looking for the Northwest Passage. In 1610 Henry Hudson had explored a large bay in the north. Later it was named Hudson Bay after him. Explorers thought they might find a route leading from Hudson Bay to the Western Ocean.

The Hudson's Bay Company Is Formed

In 1670 the Hudson's Bay Company was formed in England. The purpose of the company was to trade with the Indians for furs. The company built **trading posts** along the rivers that flowed into Hudson Bay. One of the trading posts was called York Factory. It was on the Hayes River.

Why did the Hudson's Bay Company build trading posts along rivers?

Another purpose of the Hudson's Bay Company was to explore. The land west of Hudson Bay was hard to explore. In the south, the land was covered with dense forests. In the north, the land was barren and frozen for most of the year.

Winters were long and cold. During the short summers the air was filled with clouds of mosquitoes and black flies. For many years people from the Hudson's Bay Company did not try to explore this land. They sailed ships along the coast of Hudson Bay, trading with Indians there. The people from the company also looked for an entrance to the Northwest Passage.

Then the company decided to send an explorer west into the forest. A young man named Henry Kelsey was chosen.

Kelsey Sees the Buffalo

Henry Kelsey spent a lot of his time with the Cree Indians who lived near York Factory. He learned how to speak their language. He also learned how to shoot a bow and arrow. Kelsey made several trips along the coast of Hudson Bay with the Crees. He was 20 years old when he began his journey into the forest.

Why might Henry Kelsey be a good person to go exploring in the wilderness with the Indians?

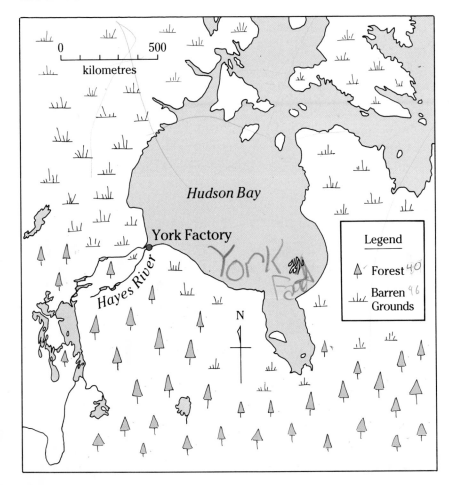

Above: At one time the prairies were filled with buffalo. Where can you see buffalo today?

Left: Kelsey made several journeys along the coast of Hudson Bay. What is the land like there?

55

Above: Kelsey sees the buffalo on the prairies. What might happen next?

Right: The buffalo used to rub up against rocks like this one. Why do you think the buffalo did that?

In the spring of 1690 Kelsey left York Factory with a group of Cree Indians. They walked across the barren land around York Factory until they reached the forest. Then they travelled by canoe through the forest. At last they reached the prairies. The land was covered with thick grass. Herds of buffalo grazed there. Kelsey was the first European to see the buffalo on the Canadian prairies.

Next Kelsey went south across the prairies to the land of the Assiniboine Indians. He travelled and hunted buffalo with them. To hunt the buffalo, the Assiniboines surrounded a buffalo herd and gradually moved closer and closer. When they were close enough, the Assiniboines shot their arrows and threw their spears at the buffalo.

Kelsey was gone for almost two years. When he got back to York Factory, he gave a report on what he had seen. He said the Indians had many good furs. The Hudson's Bay Company did not want to travel a long way to trade with the Indians. The company liked the Indians to come to the forts. As a result, it was many years before another explorer journeyed from Hudson Bay to the prairies.

The La Vérendryes See the Mountains

Most of Canada's explorers were born in France or in Great Britain. Pierre Gaultier de Varennes, Sieur de la Vérendrye, was different. He was born in Canada, in the town of Trois-Rivières.

La Vérendrye had four sons. When they grew up, they went with their father to explore the wilderness west of the Great Lakes. Like the other explorers, the La Vérendryes wanted to find a route to the Western Ocean. They also wanted to get furs.

How was La Vérendrye different from the other explorers you have learned about? How was he the same?

In 1731, La Vérendrye left Montreal with three of his sons. A group of **voyageurs** and Indian interpreters went with them in their canoes. It took the explorers all summer to get to the woods north of Lake Superior. During the journey they ate cornmeal mush. They also caught fish and hunted for deer and moose. The journey was hard, but the voyageurs sang as they paddled their canoes.

Who Were the Voyageurs?

The voyageurs were French-Canadians who paddled canoes for the fur trading companies. They were so skilled at paddling through the swift rivers that they had very few accidents. They also knew how to build and repair canoes.

The voyageurs were strong and hardy. They often paddled from early in the morning until late at night. When they had to make a portage, each man carried a 45 kg (kilogram) pack.

Despite the hardships, the voyageurs had their pleasures. They often sang songs as they paddled, keeping time with their paddles. For a break, the voyageurs would stop to smoke their pipes for a few minutes. Then they would go back to the hard work of paddling their canoes.

The next year, the La Vérendryes continued their journey west. They were guided by the Cree and the Monsoni Indians. The La Vérendryes built trading posts as they went. At last the La Vérendryes and the Indians reached Lake Winnipeg. Now they were on the edge of the prairies.

La Vérendrye had heard of some Indians called the Mandans who lived in villages in the south. He decided to visit them. A group of Indians guided La Vérendrye and the other French explorers to the Mandan country. The group included men, women and children. Winter was coming, so they took lots of blankets, leggings and mittens with them.

The explorers journeyed south into a region that is now part of the United States. At last they came to the Mandan villages. The Mandans gave La Vérendrye a feast. They told him about their country. They also told La Vérendrye about some people who lived far in the west on the shores of a saltwater sea. La Vérendrye thought that sea might be the Western Ocean. He decided that he would try to find a route to the sea on his next journey.

Why did La Vérendrye want to find a route to the Western Ocean?

Page 58: This picture shows the area where the La Vérendryes were travelling. What do you think it would be like to paddle along this lake?

Below: The La Vérendryes went from Lake Winnipeg to Mandan country. In what direction were they travelling?

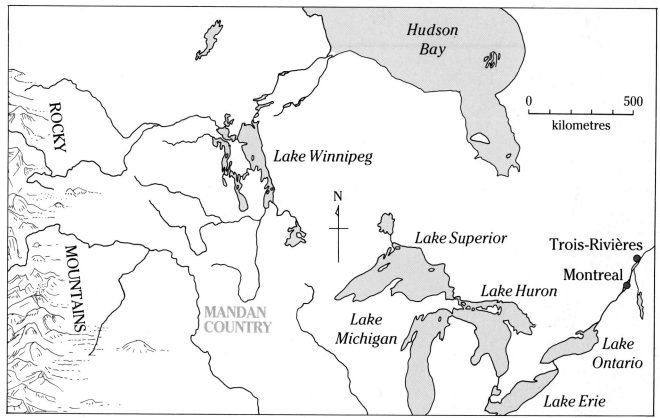

La Vérendrye and his companions left the Mandan villages to go home. Winter had now set in. Thick snow covered the prairies. La Vérendrye and the Indians walked through howling blizzards. At night they huddled in snowdrifts for shelter. La Vérendrye became very ill on that journey. He could not do any more exploring, so his sons began to explore for him.

In 1742, two of La Vérendrye's sons, François and Louis-Joseph, went back to the Mandans' country. From there they journeyed west across the prairies. They were looking for a route to the Western Ocean. We are not sure how far they travelled. They probably saw the snow-capped peaks of the Rocky Mountains.

The La Vérendryes did not find a route to the Western Ocean. They did find out more about Canada's geography.

La Vérendrye's sons approach the Rocky Mountains. How might they have felt when they saw the mountains?

60

They also built many trading posts. Two of La Vérendrye's sons, François and Louis-Joseph, were probably the first people besides the Indians to see the Rocky Mountains.

What Have We Learned?

Young Henry Kelsey journeyed from Hudson Bay to the prairies. He was the first European to see the buffalo in Canada.

The La Vérendryes journeyed to Lake Winnipeg. They built trading posts along the way. Then they went south across the prairies. Two of La Vérendrye's sons probably saw the Rocky Mountains in what is now the United States.

This map shows the routes that Kelsey and the La Vérendryes took on their journeys. How many trading posts can you find on the map?

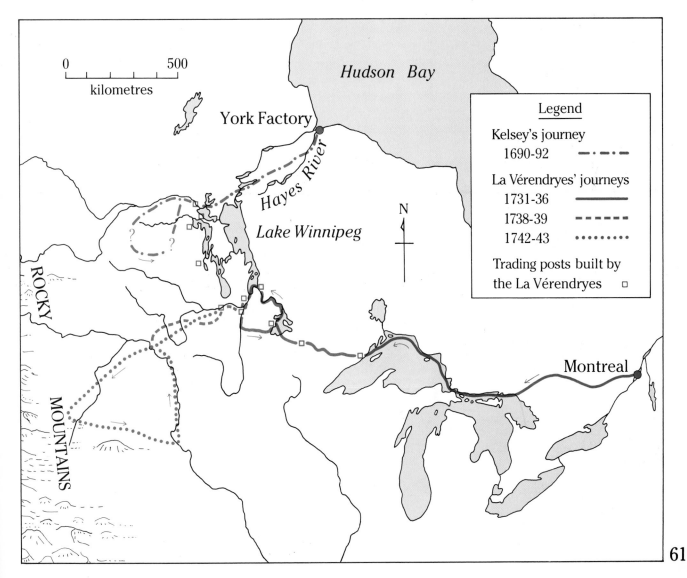

Anthony Henday Crosses the Prairies

What Lies Ahead?

In this part of the chapter, you will find out the answers to these questions.

- Who was Anthony Henday?

- What was Henday looking for when he crossed the prairies?

- How did the Indians help Henday?

- What new things did Henday find out about the prairies?

Who Was Anthony Henday?

Not much is known about Anthony Henday. He was born on the Isle of Wight, off the south coast of England. He was trained to be a sailor. Later Henday joined the Hudson's Bay Company and came to Canada. He worked at York Factory as a net maker. A man who knew him there wrote that Henday was bold and enterprising.

It had taken explorers from Europe almost 300 years to get from the Atlantic Ocean to the prairies. They had followed rivers and lakes used by the Indians for many hundreds of years. Slowly the explorers had moved through the forest. Now they were on the prairies. Some of the early explorers called the prairies the Muscuty Plains. Muscuty comes from the Cree word *muskootao*, which means "wide prairies or plains."

The Crees who lived around York Factory told the traders there about Indians who lived far away on the prairies. These Indians rode horses and had many furs. They were called the Blackfoot.

The Hudson's Bay Company decided to send a man to visit the Blackfoot. He would ask the Blackfoot chief to send some Indians to trade their furs at York Factory.

The young man who volunteered to look for the Blackfoot was Anthony Henday. A group of Crees would go with him. In June of 1754 they set off by canoe up the Hayes River into the forest. Henday kept a **journal** telling of his travels, and that is how we know what happened.

What kind of things do you think an explorer might write about in a journal?

Page 62: Henday and the Crees set out along the Hayes River. What might they be carrying in the bundles?

Who Was Grey Goose Woman?

Grey Goose Woman is the name we have given to the Cree woman who went with Henday on his journey. She was probably only 17 or 18 years old. Even so, she knew how to prepare skins and how to cut and sew them into fine clothes. She also knew how to decorate the shirts and moccasins with porcupine quills.

While Henday lived with the Crees, Grey Goose Woman was his teacher. She showed Henday how to live with her people. She taught Henday the customs of the Crees.

Page 65: Grey Goose Woman tells the story of her journey with Henday. Do you like to hear people tell stories?

The group of Crees who went with Henday included several women. Cree women always went on the journeys. They did the cooking and prepared the animal skins. The most important job a woman had was making clothes and moccasins. Without warm clothes, people could easily die in the long, cold winters.

One of the Cree women prepared Henday's meals and made his clothes. We do not know that woman's name. Let us find a name for her. We will call her Grey Goose Woman.

Why was it important for Cree women to go along on the journeys?

Journey to the Prairies

Let us imagine that many years have passed since Grey Goose Woman journeyed with Henday. She is an old woman now. It is a winter evening, and some Cree families are sitting around the fire listening to stories of long ago. It is Grey Goose Woman's turn to talk. Everyone is quiet while she speaks.

The Story of Grey Goose Woman

Long ago, some of our people and a man from York Factory journeyed far across the prairies to see the Blackfoot people. This man was called Anthony Henday. He wanted the Blackfoot to bring their furs to York Factory. The traders there said they would give the Blackfoot many fine things for their furs. Chief Little Deer said we would take Henday to speak to the Blackfoot chief.

We started out from York Factory in our canoes. It was summer. The river was shallow and filled with rocks. We had to carry our canoes through deep swamps and over sharp rocks.

We didn't find many fish in the river. Sometimes we killed a duck or a few beaver, but that wasn't very much food. We were often hungry. We were also tired from taking our canoes over so many portages.

Finally we came to a big lake surrounded by tall pines and birch trees. The lake was filled with fish. We caught many pike and killed three ducks there. It was good to have enough to eat.

As they travelled, Henday and the Cree Indians lived mostly on fish. They caught the fish with nets when they camped at the end of the day. It took the travellers almost a month to reach the Saskatchewan River. At last they came to Fort Paskoyac, which La Vérendrye's sons had built. Some French fur traders lived at the fort.

The Story of Grey Goose Woman

When we got to Fort Paskoyac, the Frenchmen there asked Henday where he was going. He told them he had come to explore the country. The Frenchmen said he could not go on. Henday went to Little Deer and told him what the Frenchmen had said. Little Deer smiled. He knew the Frenchmen could not stop us from taking Henday where we wanted.

Henday gave the Frenchmen a long piece of tobacco. They did not have good tobacco. The gift of tobacco pleased the Frenchmen, and they invited Henday to eat with them. Then they gave him some moose meat to take with him on his journey.

The next day we left Fort Paskoyac. Soon we would be with the rest of our people again. The children and the old people had been left in a camp near the Peatago River. They were not strong enough to make a journey through the forest to York

On the first part of their journey, Henday and the Crees travelled in their canoes from York Factory to the Peatago River. What is this river called today?

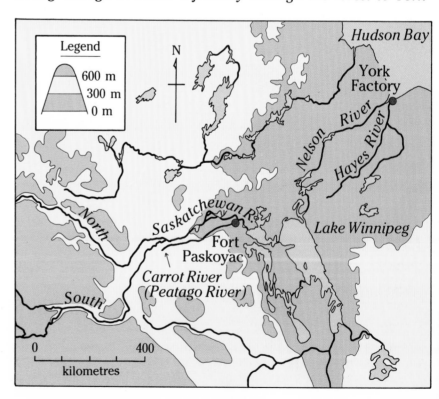

Factory. We had not seen them for a long time. So we hurried up the Saskatchewan River until we came to the Peatago River. For two days we paddled as fast as we could along the river. At last we came to the place where we always left our canoes. Now we would begin our walk towards the prairies.

Henday and the Crees unloaded their packs from the canoes and put them on their backs. Then they set off on foot, leaving the canoes behind. After walking a few kilometres, they arrived at the camp where the Crees had left the children and the old people.

The Story of Grey Goose Woman

When we got to the camp, we found that our people were starving. They had not been able to find food while we were gone. The children were nothing but skin and bones. We were hungry, too, for we had not had much to eat for several days. That night we all went to sleep with empty stomachs.

The next day we walked on towards the prairies. One day passed. There was not a bird or animal to be seen. The children cried because they had nothing to eat.

We kept on walking. At last we came to a meadow that was filled with ripe strawberries. We dropped to our knees and began eating them. They tasted good after so many days of almost nothing to eat. We ate our fill of berries. Then we were at peace because we had eaten well.

Henday and Grey Goose Woman saw many chokecherry trees.

Henday and the Crees were getting close to the prairies. As they came to the end of the forest, they saw small clumps of chokecherry trees, hazelnut bushes, poplars and willows. Henday and the Cree hunters found plenty of moose and elk to shoot for their food.

At last they reached the prairies. There the land was flat and covered with thick grass. Except for a few small chokecherry and birch trees, there were no woods. A few small ponds were scattered about, but the water in them was not very good for drinking.

About a week after reaching the prairies, Henday and the Crees came to the South Saskatchewan River. They had travelled over 1000 km (kilometres) from York Factory.

What are the different ways Henday and the Crees travelled from York Factory?

INTERIOR
PLAINS

The Interior Plains

The Interior Plains make up a large part of Canada. Henday and the Crees travelled through the southern part of this region. The pictures help you see what the Interior Plains look like today.

Long ago, in the time of the dinosaurs, the Interior Plains were covered with warm, shallow seas. The land we see today was once the bottom of those seas. The plains are mostly flat land. In some places there are low hills.

Large rivers flow north or east across the Interior Plains. Indians and explorers paddled canoes along them. This region has only a few very large lakes, but there are many shallow

Top: The South Saskatchewan River flows through the Interior Plains.

Bottom: Coniferous forests grow in the northern part of the Interior Plains. You can see bogs and lakes there, too.

sloughs. Sloughs are low places in the ground that fill up with water from rain or melting snow. Often they dry up in summer.

If you were exploring the Interior Plains, you would go through two areas. The northern area is mainly forest, and the southern area is the prairies. Before Henday reached the prairies, he travelled through a small part of the forest.

The thick forest thins out towards the north. There it includes some patches of grassland and wet bogs. The forest has not changed much since Henday's time.

When Henday was exploring, the prairies were covered with grass. Some grass was tall, and some was short. The grass was taller in the east, where there was more rainfall. Grass was an important food for animals such as the buffalo.

Imagine following Henday's route through the prairies today. The region has changed from long ago. Buffalo no longer roam the prairies. When settlers plowed the grass to plant crops, there was no longer enough food for the buffalo. Today you would see many grain farms instead of grass. Wheat is the most important crop.

Most of the people in the Interior Plains live on the prairies. Some are farmers, but many live in cities, too.

Left: Today there are many wheat farms on the prairies.

Left: Pronghorn antelope live on the prairies.

Right: You can see many shallow sloughs in the Interior Plains.

The Crees are making canoes out of moose skins so that they can cross the South Saskatchewan River. Why didn't they bring canoes with them on the journey?

70

The Story of Grey Goose Woman

The river was so deep and wide that we could not wade across it. The men had to make skin boats. They cut willow branches from shrubs along the banks and made them into frames. Then they put moose skins over each frame. While the men were making the skin boats, the women picked berries on the river banks. The berries were big and juicy.

Henday sat by the river fishing. He caught several trout. We roasted the fish over a fire and ate them with the berries. Then we paddled in the skin boats across the river and walked on over the prairies towards the setting sun.

Why did the Crees make their boats out of moose skins?

Henday and the Crees began to see large herds of buffalo. Sometimes there were so many buffalo that the explorers had to make them move out of the way. Each herd of buffalo was followed by wolves and sometimes by grizzly bears. These predatory animals fed on the old buffalo and the calves.

Right: Henday and the Crees crossed the South Saskatchewan River. Then they continued walking west. What might they see after reaching Blackfoot country?

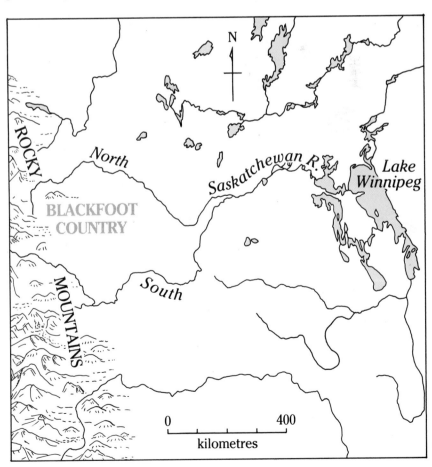

The Story of Grey Goose Woman

Henday was amazed when the first big herd of buffalo came along. He could not believe how many there were. Our hunters killed several buffalo, and we cooked the tongues and humps.

On the prairies we saw many animals. We saw antelope, wild horses, moose, beavers and snakes. Above us flew eagles, magpies, pigeons and woodpeckers. Henday said he had never seen so many animals before.

One day a grizzly bear attacked two of our young men. They were out hunting buffalo. When the hunters saw the bear, they thought they would be able to kill it. Instead, they only wounded it, and the bear attacked them. One of the hunters died. It is hard to win a fight against a grizzly.

Arrival in Blackfoot Country

Some days Henday and the Crees did not travel. Instead the men went hunting and the women dried buffalo meat. One day they stopped so that the women could prepare skins for moccasins. Suddenly they heard a shout. The men jumped up and stared over the prairies. Coming towards them were two men riding horses.

At last Henday and the Crees had reached the country of the Blackfoot Indians.

The Story of Grey Goose Woman

The two Blackfoot riders did not stay long. They said that their great chief was several days' journey away.

Two days later a group of Blackfoot came to stay with us. The men were all on horseback. Henday gave them some tobacco and smoked a pipe with them. The leader pointed to smoke in the sky far across the prairies. He said it came from the Blackfoot camp. Then the Blackfoot got on their horses and rode off across the prairies towards the distant smoke.

For 12 more days Henday and the Crees walked across the prairies. Now they were close to the Rocky Mountains.

Henday and the Crees passed great herds of buffalo. They saw more antelope and moose and beaver. What a wonderful place the prairies must have been when Anthony Henday was there in 1754.

The grizzly bear can be dangerous. Why might a grizzly attack a person?

At last Henday and Chief Little Deer were visited by seven Blackfoot Indians. They told Henday that he would meet their great chief the next day.

What might Henday say to the Blackfoot chief when they meet?

The Story of Grey Goose Woman

It was a grand occasion when we set out to visit the great chief of the Blackfoot people. In front rode four Blackfoot warriors. Then came Little Deer and our other chiefs. The rest of us walked behind.

At last we came to the Blackfoot camp. There were 200 teepees, set in two rows. We walked down the long path between the two rows, where the Blackfoot people stood watching us. At the far end was the great chief's teepee. It was so big that 50 people could fit into it. The great chief was sitting in the middle of the teepee on a buffalo skin. Other Blackfoot chiefs sat all around him.

Henday enters the Blackfoot camp. What might the Blackfoot Indians be thinking?

The great chief motioned for Henday to sit on his right side. Then Henday and the Blackfoot chiefs smoked a pipe. After that, baskets of buffalo meat were passed around. Henday was given a basket holding 10 tongues to take with him.

Little Deer interpreted for Henday. He told the great chief that Henday brought a message from the great leader at York Factory. The great leader wanted the Blackfoot to bring their wolf skins and beaver skins to the fort. In exchange they would get cloth and beads and many other things the great leader had at York Factory.

The Blackfoot chief did not talk much. He said only that York Factory was far away and the Blackfoot had no canoes. Then he and Little Deer and Henday talked of other things. At last the Blackfoot chief told us it was time to leave, and we walked back to our camp.

Henday stayed with the Blackfoot Indians for several more days. He visited the great chief again. Once more Henday asked him to send some of his people to York Factory to trade with the Hudson's Bay Company. The great chief replied that the Blackfoot people needed their horses and could not leave them. Nor could they live without the buffalo. The herds of buffalo gave them everything they needed—food, clothes, homes, and saddles and bridles for their horses.

The great chief told Henday that his people were not like the Crees. They did not eat fish. They did not know how to make and paddle canoes. The Blackfoot did not want to take their furs to York Factory. Then Henday gave the great chief the presents he had brought from York Factory. In return the great chief gave Henday a fine bow and some arrows.

Why didn't the Blackfoot want to go to York Factory to trade?

Soon the Blackfoot took down their teepees and followed the buffalo herds. Winter was coming. Henday and the Crees began to prepare for the long, cold winter ahead of them.

The Blackfoot chief is telling Henday to sit on his right side. What is the chief sitting on?

How the Crees Prepared for Winter

For winter the Crees and Henday needed warm clothing, snowshoes and toboggans. The Cree women made the clothes. This was something they did all year round. Preparing animal skins for clothing was hard work. It took up much of every Cree woman's time.

When it was very cold, the Crees wore robes made of hides with the hair or fur left on. The robe could be a single skin, such as a buffalo skin or a deer skin. Or it could be several small skins, such as beaver, sewn together with **sinew**. Henday and the Crees

To make clothes, first the animal had to be skinned. Next the hide was staked to the ground or stretched on a rack. Then any bits of fat and meat were scraped off the hide. The hide was dried in the sun. Then it was rubbed with a mixture of animal brains and fat. The skin was left to dry again. Then it was rubbed and worked until it was soft. When the hides were ready, they were sewn together to make a robe.

Sinew was used to sew the hides together.

wore clothes made of beaver fur when the weather got cold.

While the women made the clothing, the men made the snowshoes and toboggans. A person wearing snowshoes would not sink into the snow. The Crees pulled their supplies over the snow on toboggans. The front ends of the toboggans were turned up so they would glide easily over the snow.

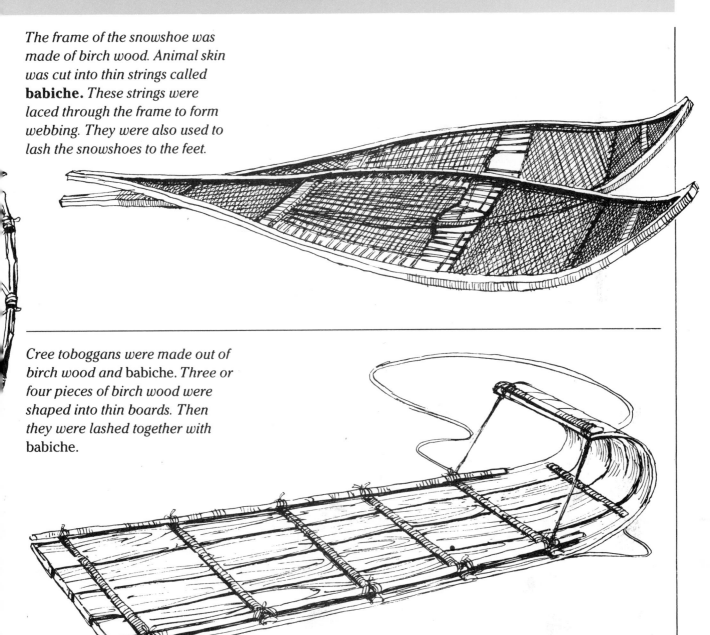

The frame of the snowshoe was made of birch wood. Animal skin was cut into thin strings called **babiche.** *These strings were laced through the frame to form webbing. They were also used to lash the snowshoes to the feet.*

Cree toboggans were made out of birch wood and babiche. *Three or four pieces of birch wood were shaped into thin boards. Then they were lashed together with* babiche.

The Journey Home

After leaving the Blackfoot camp, Henday and the Crees moved west. They left the open prairies. They travelled to the tree-filled valleys at the foot of the Rocky Mountains.

The Story of Grey Goose Woman

When snow began to fall, we moved from the open plains into the forest, where the tall trees sheltered us. We stopped travelling for a few days so that the women could make clothing and moccasins. The men made toboggans and snowshoes out of birch wood.

One day Henday asked me why the Crees did not trap wolves and beaver. He said there were many beaver in the streams waiting to be trapped. He was angry because he wanted to take furs with him back to York Factory.

I told Henday that the Cree people did not trap beaver and wolves in Blackfoot country. We were traders like the men who lived at York Factory. The Blackfoot did not mind if we killed buffalo to eat. They did not mind if we killed a few beaver and wolves to make into warm winter clothes. But they did not want us to kill their beaver and wolves to trade. If we did, they would be angry. I told Henday that he did not have to worry. In the spring, we would bring him many canoe loads of furs from the Blackfoot people.

Why didn't the Blackfoot want the Crees to kill many wolves and beaver in Blackfoot country?

When winter came, the Crees changed from their leather clothes into warmer clothes made of beaver furs. Slowly Henday and the Cree Indians made their way to the North Saskatchewan River. When the ice melted they would begin the long canoe trip back to York Factory.

Henday saw many beavers on the prairies. Can you see why beaver fur would make warm clothing?

Henday and the Crees are walking towards the Rocky Mountains. Why do they want to leave the prairies?

The Story of Grey Goose Woman

At last the time of the open water came. The snow began to melt. The ice on the river softened and cracked. Geese and swans filled the sky. It was time to begin building the canoes. We worked hard during the day. At night we feasted and danced.

The day came when we were ready to put our canoes into the river. We loaded our bundles, climbed in and dipped our paddles into the water. Henday shouted, "We're off!" He began to sing, and I raised my voice to join him. We had begun our long journey back to York Factory.

What Happened to Grey Goose Woman?

No one knows what happened to Grey Goose Woman after she returned to York Factory. Perhaps she married and had children. We can imagine Grey Goose Woman sitting and sewing moccasins. Her baby might be sleeping in the sunshine in its cradle of birch bark and deer skin. Perhaps the baby's older brother and sister are playing in the grass nearby. As Grey Goose Woman draws the thread through the moccasins, she listens to the sounds of her children playing. Perhaps Grey Goose Woman is remembering the days when she journeyed across the prairies with Anthony Henday.

What Happened to Anthony Henday?

Henday reached York Factory on June 20, 1755. He had been gone a year.

Very little is known about Henday after he returned to York Factory. We do know that Henday returned to the Blackfoot country once again. After that, Henday left the Hudson's Bay Company and went back to England.

Perhaps it does not matter that so little is known about what happened to Henday. What matters is that this bold and enterprising man was the first European explorer to cross the Canadian prairies. That is why Canadians will always remember the name of Anthony Henday.

Henday and the Crees will soon be heading back to York Factory. How are they preparing for the journey back?

What Have We Learned?

Henry Kelsey and the La Vérendryes explored the prairies. Kelsey went from York Factory to the prairies. Pierre Gaultier de Varennes, Sieur de la Vérendrye, also journeyed to the prairies. He built trading posts. Two of his sons went across the American prairies, probably as far as the Rocky Mountains. Later, Anthony Henday crossed the Canadian prairies. He went as far as the **foothills** of the Rocky Mountains.

Unlike the other explorers, Anthony Henday was not looking for the Northwest Passage. He went across the prairies to visit the Blackfoot Indians. He wanted them to bring their furs to the Hudson's Bay Company to trade.

Henday travelled to the prairies with a group of Cree Indians. While they were travelling, he lived with them as part of their community. Almost everything Henday used during his journey was made by the Cree Indians. He travelled in a birch-bark canoe made by the Cree men. A Cree woman cooked his food and made his clothes and moccasins. Without the help of the Indians, Henday could never have made his great journey across the prairies.

Henday found the Blackfoot Indians following the great herds of buffalo close to the foothills of the Rocky Mountains. His journey across the prairies brought the explorers one step closer to the Western Ocean. Henday had gone farther west in Canada than any European before him.

In this chapter we have learned about the exploration of the prairies from 1690 to 1755.

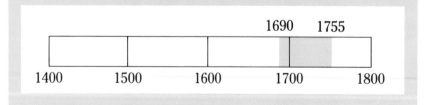

This map shows the route that Henday took on his journey. On his way back to York Factory, what river did he follow first?

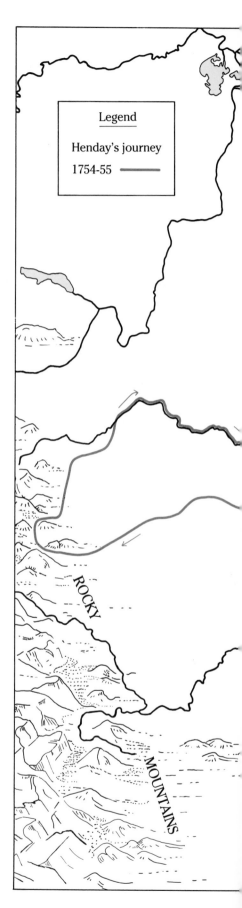

Legend

Henday's journey
1754-55 ———

ROCKY MOUNTAINS

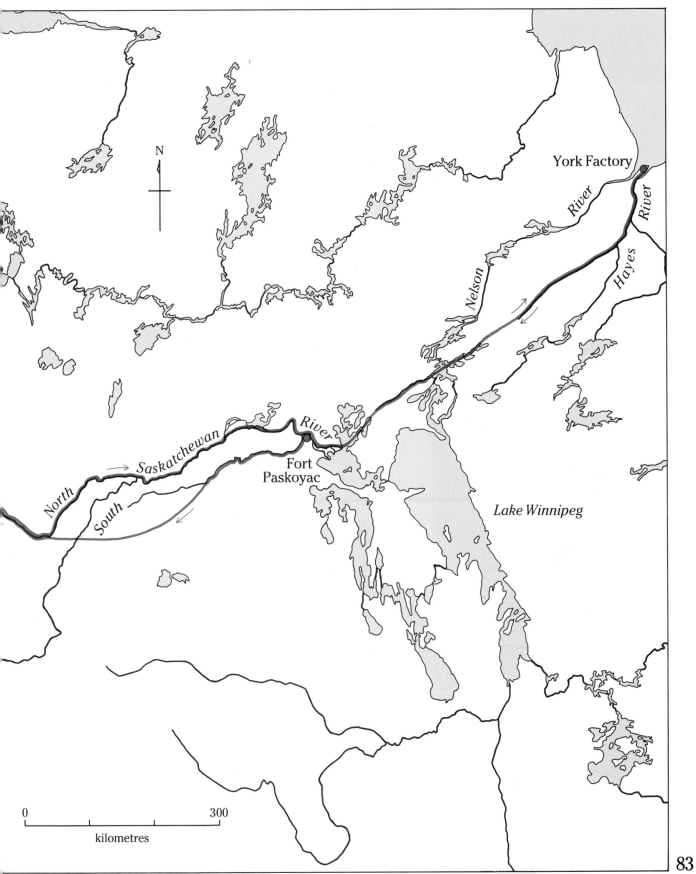

York Factory

Nelson River

Hayes River

North

South

Saskatchewan River

Fort Paskoyac

Lake Winnipeg

N

0   300
kilometres

Two Points of View

The Blackfoot lived on the prairies for a long time. They depended on the prairie animals. Then the fur traders came. They saw the same animals, but they didn't feel the same way the Blackfoot felt about them. The Blackfoot and the fur traders looked at the animals from different points of view.

Eagle Woman, a Blackfoot Indian

I like to see the herds of buffalo grazing on the prairies. My people need the buffalo and the other animals. The animals give us food, clothing and shelter. Wherever the buffalo herds go, we follow. To me, the prairie animals mean life. Without them, my people could not survive. Our hunters kill only as many animals as we need. We always leave enough animals for the next hunt.

Why were the prairie animals important to Eagle Woman?

Joseph White, Fur Trader

I travelled across the prairies and saw huge herds of buffalo. Buffalo fur is ugly. We could not sell it in Europe. There are also many beavers on the prairies. Their fur is very beautiful. We can make a lot of money selling beaver furs in Europe. We should get as many beaver furs as we can. Fur prices are high in Europe. In the future, prices may drop. We should make a profit while we can.

Why were the prairie animals important to Joseph White?

Looking Back

Explorers and Their Achievements

Match the explorers in the first list with the achievements in the second list.

Explorers	Achievements

Explorers

a. Henry Kelsey
b. La Vérendrye
c. Anthony Henday

Achievements

1. I went from York Factory to the foothills of the Rocky Mountains.
2. I went from Montreal to the prairies.
3. I went from Hudson Bay to the prairies.
4. I built trading posts west of Lake Superior.

How the Indians Helped

Henday dressed as the Crees did when he was travelling across the prairies. Draw a picture of what you think he looked like in his winter gear. Explain how these clothes helped Henday.

Geography of the Interior Plains

The climate of the Interior Plains made exploring difficult. Look back through the chapter to find sentences that describe the climate.

Imagine You Were There

What would you have said or done —
  if you saw a herd of buffalo for the first time?
  if you were asked to cross a river in a boat made of animal hides?
  if you were a Blackfoot chief and Henday asked you to bring furs to York Factory?

Find Out More

1. Go to your library and find out how the Plains Indians used the buffalo. Draw a picture showing some of the ways buffalo were used.
2. Henday was a fur trader for the Hudson's Bay Company. Go to the library and see what you can find out about the early fur traders in Canada. Write a paragraph about the life of the early fur traders.
3. In this chapter you have learned that dinosaurs roamed the Interior Plains long ago. Find out what kind of dinosaurs used to live in this region. Draw a picture of some of these dinosaurs.

4

Who Explored the Barren Grounds?

Samuel Hearne Crosses the Barren Grounds

Each explorer added more information to the map of Canada. Anthony Henday had put the prairies on the map. The next part of Canada to be explored was the large region farther north. First there was forest northeast of the prairies. Beyond that was an area where it was too cold for trees to grow. This area was called the Barren Grounds.

The next part of Canada to be explored was the region north of the prairies. How does the land change as you go farther north?

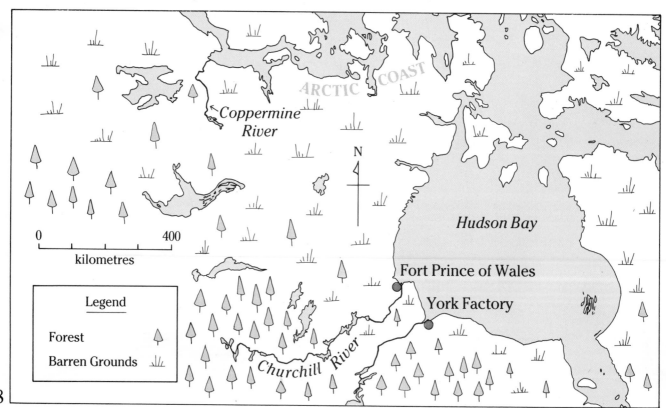

ARCTIC COAST

Coppermine River

N

Hudson Bay

Fort Prince of Wales

York Factory

0   400
kilometres

Legend

Forest   🌲

Barren Grounds ⱵⱵ

Churchill River

The Hudson's Bay Company had built a trading post at the mouth of the Churchill River. The trading post was called Fort Prince of Wales. Each year Chipewyan Indians came to Fort Prince of Wales to trade their furs. Sometimes they brought lumps of copper to the fort. They said the copper came from a mine beside a river far to the north. The Hudson's Bay Company called this river the Coppermine River.

The traders wanted to find the copper mine. They wanted to find out if ships could sail up the Coppermine River to the copper mine. The Hudson's Bay Company also wanted to find the Northwest Passage. The traders hoped that ships could travel from Hudson Bay to the Arctic Ocean. They hoped that the Coppermine River was part of the Northwest Passage.

The Hudson's Bay Company decided to send someone to explore the Barren Grounds. The explorer that the company chose was a young man named Samuel Hearne.

Hearne's First Journey

Hearne did not get very far on his first journey into the Barren Grounds. He went with two other men from the Hudson's Bay Company. Their guide was a Cree Indian. Several other Crees and some Chipewyan men and women also went on the journey. None of them knew how to get to the copper mine.

Hearne and the Indians set out early in November of 1769. After a few days, they reached the Barren Grounds. The land was bare, except for some rocks and stones and a few small trees scattered here and there. The weather was very cold. Hearne and the Indians had trouble finding firewood. Their toboggans kept breaking on the stones, and it was difficult to find wood to use for repairs. The explorers also had trouble finding caribou to eat.

Finally the Indians decided to go home. They didn't know how much longer it would take them to get to the copper mine. They wanted to go back to their families.

After the Indians went off into the forest, Hearne and his two friends turned back towards the fort. Most of the time they had little to eat. Some days each man had only half a partridge to eat. Other days they had nothing. At last the three men arrived at Fort Prince of Wales. They had been gone one month.

Who Was Samuel Hearne?

Samuel Hearne was born in London, England, in 1745. When he was only 11 he joined the British Navy as a captain's servant. It was a hard, dangerous life. While he was in the navy, his ship fought two battles against the French.

Hearne stayed in the navy for seven years. In 1766 he joined the Hudson's Bay Company and came to Canada. There he worked on the company ship that sailed around Hudson Bay in the summer. He traded with the Indians and the Inuit who lived along the shores. Hearne was 24 when he set out to look for the copper mine. Later he published a journal describing all the things he saw along the way. His journal is still read today.

Hearne's Second Journey

Hearne spent two months at Fort Prince of Wales. In February 1770 he set out once again to look for the copper mine and the Northwest Passage. Three Chipewyans and two Crees went along as Hearne's guides. No women were on this journey.

This time Hearne and the Indians decided not to go onto the Barren Grounds so soon. Instead, they followed a river through the forest. The hunters had trouble finding caribou. Hearne and the Indians decided to camp by a lake, where they could catch fish. Then they would continue on to the Barren Grounds when the weather got warmer.

At last spring came. Hearne and the Indians began walking again. When they got to the Barren Grounds, there were no caribou. For several days the explorers had to eat scraps of leather and burned bones they found in old campfires. If they were lucky, they found dried-up cranberries to eat. It rained so hard that the explorers could not even make a fire with the moss that grows on the Barren Grounds.

Then one day a strong gust of wind knocked over Hearne's **quadrant** and broke it. Without a quadrant, Hearne could not measure the **latitude**. He could not draw a map to show where he had been.

Once more Samuel Hearne had to return to Fort Prince of Wales. On his way back, Hearne met a group of Chipewyan Indians. They were going to the fort to trade their furs. The leader was Matonabbee. The first thing Matonabbee did was give Hearne a warm suit made from the skins of otters and other animals. Then Matonabbee told Hearne that he would never be able to cross the Barren Grounds without the help of women. Matonabbee offered to be Hearne's guide on his next journey to the copper mine. He also told Hearne that Chipewyan women would go with them.

At last Hearne got back to Fort Prince of Wales. He had been gone more than eight months.

What problems did Hearne have on his second journey into the Barren Grounds? What was the reason he decided to go back to Fort Prince of Wales?

Hearne meets Matonabbee on the way back to Fort Prince of Wales. What might Matonabbee be saying to Hearne?

Who Was Matonabbee?

Matonabbee was a Chipewyan Indian. He was born around 1736. When his father died, he was adopted by one of the men at Fort Prince of Wales. Matonabbee lived at the fort for several years. There he learned to speak English and Cree.

Hearne wrote in his journal that Matonabbee was tall and handsome. Matonabbee was also brave. When he was still a youth, he brought about peace between the Chipewyans and their neighbours. The two tribes had been at war for a long time. In 1769 Matonabbee travelled to the copper mine with another Indian leader. Matonabbee knew how to get to the copper mine and became Hearne's guide.

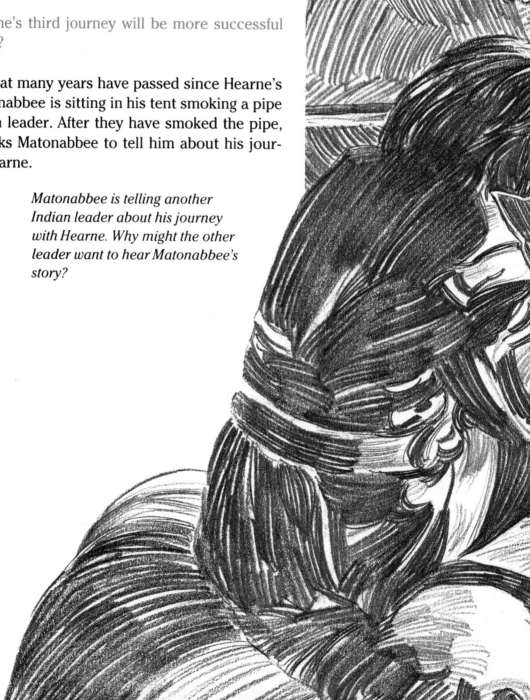

Hearne's Third Journey

Samuel Hearne left Fort Prince of Wales for the third time in December of 1770. Matonabbee and a group of Chipewyans were with him. Once more Hearne was going to look for the copper mine and the Northwest Passage. This time he was with Indians who knew how to get to the copper mine. This time there were women along to cook and to make clothes and moccasins from caribou skins.

Do you think Hearne's third journey will be more successful than his other ones?

Let us pretend that many years have passed since Hearne's third journey. Matonabbee is sitting in his tent smoking a pipe with another Indian leader. After they have smoked the pipe, the other Indian asks Matonabbee to tell him about his journey with Samuel Hearne.

Matonabbee is telling another Indian leader about his journey with Hearne. Why might the other leader want to hear Matonabbee's story?

92

Matonabbee's Story

Our journey began slowly. One of our people was sick and had to be pulled on a toboggan. To make things worse, when we got to the Barren Grounds we couldn't find any caribou to eat. For days we had nothing but a pipe of tobacco and a drink of snow water. Still, we walked from morning until night. You know what it's like when you can't find food. You laugh and make jokes and tease each other. It doesn't help to be sad when things aren't going well for you.

After many days on the Barren Grounds, we moved back into the forest. Soon we found a herd of caribou. The hunters killed some of them and we had a feast. You know how it is. When you have plenty of food, you eat and eat until you can't eat any more. You never know how long it will be until you have food again.

Hearne and the Chipewyans were following herds of caribou like this one. Why do you think caribou travel in herds?

94

Why do you think the Chipewyans laughed and made jokes when they didn't have enough to eat?

Hearne and the Chipewyans were travelling west. They had crossed a stretch of the Barren Grounds and then had moved back into the forest. The Chipewyans knew they would find caribou there, since the caribou travelled through the forest in winter. When spring came, the caribou would go north across the Barren Grounds. By following the caribou, Hearne and the Chipewyans would be sure to have enough to eat.

Sometimes Hearne asked Matonabbee if they could travel a little faster through the forest. Matonabbee told Hearne they must stay with the caribou. It would be better to cross the Barren Grounds to the copper mine in the summer. Then the caribou would also be crossing the Barren Grounds.

The caribou has large antlers. What might be hanging from this caribou's antlers?

95

The Canadian Shield

CANADIAN SHIELD

The Canadian Shield is the largest region in Canada. It takes up about half the country. As you can see on the map, it is shaped like a giant horseshoe. Hearne explored part of the Canadian Shield. The pictures show this region today.

All of Canada is built on top of ancient rock. In some places, this very old rock is hidden deep below the surface. In the Canadian Shield, this rock lies near the surface. Some of the rock contains **minerals** such as gold and copper.

Left: Many rivers flow through the Canadian Shield. You can see how rocky the Canadian Shield is in this picture.

Right: Logging is important in the southern part of the region.

The Canadian Shield has lots of rivers, lakes and **muskeg**. Muskeg is like a giant sponge made up of moss and water. Canada has more muskeg than any other country in the world. Most of it is found in the Canadian Shield.

The northern and southern parts of the Canadian Shield are quite different. Coniferous forest covers the southern part. As you go farther north, the trees become shorter and grow farther apart. The forest ends at the **tree line**. Beyond the tree line it is too cold for trees to grow.

The area north of the tree line is called the **tundra**. Hearne called it the Barren Grounds. Just beneath the surface, the ground is always frozen. Tundra is not really barren. Some small plants grow on the frozen ground. You might see **lichen**, flowers and shrubs.

The Canadian Shield has not changed much since Hearne was there. Flowers and shrubs still grow slowly on the tundra. Only a few people live in the north, mostly in small villages. Farther south, you can still walk or paddle through the coniferous forest. Today, many of these trees are used to make paper.

The Canadian Shield is a huge region, but it does not have a lot of people. Most people there live along the southern edge. Many of the cities and towns are close to mining and lumber camps.

Above: There are many mines in the Canadian Shield.

Left: In summer, wildflowers grow on the tundra.

Matonabbee's Story

One day we met some of our people trapping caribou in the forest. Hearne was interested, so we stopped to watch. First they cut down trees and built a big pound. Inside the pound they put traps and snares. Then they put up long fences on each side of the entrance to the pound. When everything was ready, some of the people went off and got behind the herd of caribou. Then they chased the caribou into the pound. There the caribou were caught in the snares and traps and shot by the hunters. We had a feast of fine caribou meat that night.

Hearne liked the way our people trapped caribou. He thought people who stayed in one place in the winter had a good life. They didn't go hungry like the rest of us who wandered around the country. Maybe that's true, but I would rather travel, even if I go hungry sometimes. Some people are like trees. They put down roots and stay in one place all their lives. Others are like the birds and the caribou. They wander all the time. That's how I am. Hearne was a wanderer, too. That was why we got along well together.

What kind of person makes the best explorer? Why?

When spring came, Hearne and the Chipewyans set up camp in the forest. There they dried meat and gathered wood and bark from the birch trees. Soon they would turn north onto the Barren Grounds, where there were no trees. The Chipewyans used the wood to make tent poles. The bark would be used later for canoes. There would be many rivers and lakes to cross on the way to the copper mine.

At last the ice on the lakes began to melt. When they were near the Barren Grounds, the Chipewyans set to work building the canoes. When the canoes were ready, Hearne and the Chipewyans continued northward. Soon they were back on the Barren Grounds. At one of the lakes, the women and children were left behind. Only the men would go on to the copper mine.

How did Hearne and the Chipewyans prepare for their journey across the Barren Grounds?

Matonabbee's Story

After we left the women and children, we travelled quickly. We had a long way to go. We hardly stopped to sleep.

Many days passed. At last we came to a river where the ice had melted. We used our canoes to get across. It took a long time because we had only three canoes and there were many of us.

On the other side of the river we met some Copper Indians. Many seasons had passed since I last saw their chief. He was happy to see us and gave us a feast. The Copper Indians were amazed when they saw Hearne. They had never seen a man from England before.

Some of the Copper Indians said they would go with us to the mine. Now we were ready to begin the last part of our walk.

The Indians are chasing caribou into a pound. Why would a pound be a good way to catch caribou?

It was summer when Hearne and the Indians began the last part of their journey to the copper mine. The weather was bad. The first day snow fell. The second day it snowed so hard that Hearne and the Indians couldn't see where they were going. They crawled between some rocks and sat there all day until the snow stopped falling.

The next day the travellers came to some low mountains. Hearne and the Indians often had to crawl on their hands and knees along the path through the mountains. The sharp rocks cut their moccasins and feet.

Matonabbee's Story

I thought we would never get through the mountains. They were like giant heaps of stones. Have you ever tried crossing sharp stones while rain and sleet pour down on you? We were wet all the time. We couldn't even make a fire to dry our clothes.

When we finally got through the mountains, the Copper Indians took Hearne and me to see Grizzled Bear Hill. There is a cave on the hill where female bears sleep in the winter and have their young. The bears were gone, since it was summer. Instead the hill was covered with birds. Hearne was interested in every bird and animal he saw.

*Then it got hot. The mosquitoes came out in swarms. We knew we were getting close to the Coppermine River, but we weren't sure exactly where it was. We decided to follow a small stream. We hadn't gone very far when we saw some fine caribou. Our hunters killed some caribou and used the stomach of one of them to make a **beeatee**. Then we had a great feast. I remember that feast well. For a long time before that we had eaten nothing but dried meat.*

After we had eaten the beeatee and taken a short rest, we walked on to the west and up a hill. When we got to the top of the hill, we stopped and looked. There, at last, was the Coppermine River.

What might Matonabbee be thinking when he finally saw the Coppermine River?

The Coppermine River was not very deep. It was filled with waterfalls. Ships from the Hudson's Bay Company would never be able to sail along the river. This river could not be part of the Northwest Passage.

Hearne and the Indians followed the Coppermine River north. At first they saw stunted pines and dwarf willows along the banks of the river. As they went farther north, the woods grew thinner. When Hearne and the Indians got close to the mouth of the river, they saw nothing but bare hills and marshes.

This picture shows the Coppermine River near its mouth. Can you see why ships would not be able to sail along the river?

How the Chipewyans Used the Caribou

The Chipewyans could not live without the caribou. They needed it for their food, clothing and shelter. When Hearne travelled with the Chipewyans, he, too, depended on the caribou.

The Chipewyans used every part of the caribou. The hides were used to make clothing. It took eight to eleven skins to make a suit for one person. The best time to prepare the hides was in August and September. The women made all the clothes.

Caribou hides had other uses as well. The Chipewyans made their tents out of caribou hides. They also cut hides into strips of

Women tanned the hides and cut them into pieces. Then they used sinew to sew the pieces into clothes.

A tent was made from many small skins so that it would be easy to carry.

babiche. *Babiche* was used for snowshoes, snares and fishing nets. When winter came, the Chipewyans sometimes sewed the skins of caribou legs together into toboggans.

Antlers were also used. A hunter might wear a **decoy** made of caribou antler tips tied to his belt. As he walked along, the antler tips made sounds like the clicking of caribou joints. These sounds attracted the caribou.

Caribou meat was an important food. It was usually boiled, broiled or roasted. As a special treat, the Chipewyans would make a beeatee. It was one of Hearne's favourite dishes while he was travelling with the Chipewyans.

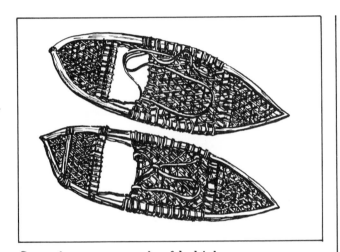

Snowshoes were made of babiche.

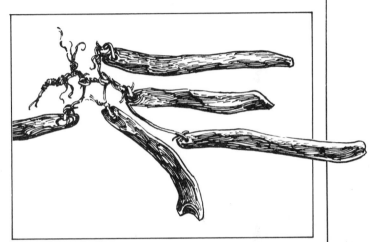

The Chipewyans used antler tips as a decoy.

A beeatee was a special treat. The stomach of a caribou was filled with caribou blood, fat and meat. Parts of the heart and lung were also added. The beeatee was then hung over the fire and roasted. When it began to steam, it was ready to eat.

103

Matonabbee's Story

At last we came to the end of the Coppermine River. There before us was the Northern Ocean. We stood on the shore and looked out across the icy water. We could see seals sleeping and playing on the ice. Hearne built a marker on the shore and claimed the land for the Hudson's Bay Company.

Then I took Hearne back up the river to the copper mine. We hunted for a long time but found only one lump of copper. Hearne was very disappointed. He put the piece of copper in his pack to take back to Fort Prince of Wales.

Hearne's job was done. He had travelled to the Arctic coast. He had seen the copper mine, although he had not seen much copper. He had found out that ships from the Hudson's Bay Company could not travel up the Coppermine River. Hearne had also found that there was no Northwest Passage through

At last Hearne and the Chipewyans reached the mouth of the Coppermine River.

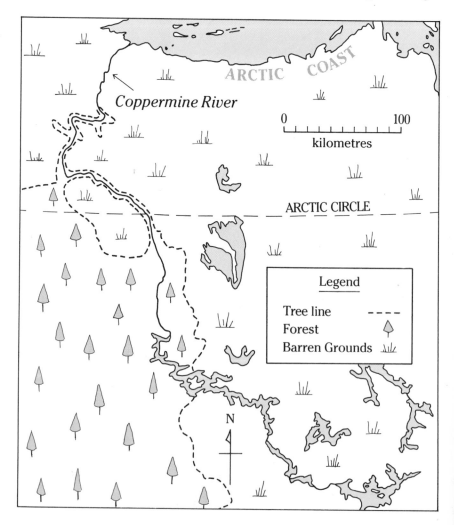

the Barren Grounds. Now it was time to begin the long journey back to Fort Prince of Wales.

What might Hearne have been feeling when he started his journey back?

Matonabbee's Story

We had no time to spare. I wanted to get back to my family. We had been gone a long time.

Off we went across the Barren Grounds. When we reached the place where we had agreed to meet the women, we found that they had left. In the distance we could see smoke from their cooking fires curling up into the sky. We hurried on towards the smoke. When we reached the smoke, we saw that it came from burning moss the women had left behind. On we went. Soon we saw more smoke. Again, when we got to the smoke, we found the women had gone. I said we must keep on walking until we reached them.

Hearne and the Chipewyans have reached the Arctic coast. What might Hearne be looking at?

105

Hearne was having a bad time. His feet were swollen and bleeding. Some of his toenails had fallen off, and the skin on his feet was raw. Still, he kept limping along, even though he left footprints of blood on the moss and the rocks.

At last we came to the women's tents. The first thing Hearne did was wash his feet. We rested for a day. After that Hearne's feet slowly got better because we weren't walking so fast.

After Hearne and the Chipewyan men had caught up with the women, several of the Indians got sick. To cure them, a shaman, or medicine man, swallowed a long piece of wood. Hearne wrote in his journal that he did not believe the man had swallowed the wood. Still, Hearne could not explain where the man had put it. Then the shaman pulled the wood out of his throat. The Chipewyans believed that the evil spirits making the people sick came out with the wood. When the sick people were well again, Hearne and the Chipewyans continued on their journey.

Matonabbee's Story

We started out across the Barren Grounds again. There were plenty of caribou. We killed a lot of them so we would have plenty of skins for warm clothes when winter came.

The lakes and rivers soon froze over. We stopped to make snowshoes and toboggans. We also dried meat to carry with us.

Snow began to fall. The days were getting short. The sun did not rise very high in the sky before it went back down again.

At last we came to the great Lake Athapuscow. It had taken us many moons to get from the Coppermine River to the lake. At the edge of the lake, we stopped to hunt caribou and beaver. Then we walked across the frozen water.

What might have happened if the explorers had not found plenty of caribou?

Hearne and the Chipewyans are on the Barren Grounds far to the north. You can see the northern lights in the sky. How are the explorers travelling?

Hearne was the first European to see Lake Athapuscow. Today it is called Great Slave Lake. When Hearne and the Chipewyans reached the south side of Great Slave Lake, they were in the forest again. In the forest Hearne saw buffalo, moose and beaver. He also saw the tracks of martens, foxes and other small animals.

Why do you think the explorers were glad to be back in the forest?

After Hearne and the Chipewyans crossed Great Slave Lake, they walked beside the Slave River. What direction were they going?

At last the explorers arrived at the Slave River. They walked along the river for several days. In January 1772, they turned away from the river and began the last part of their long journey back to Fort Prince of Wales.

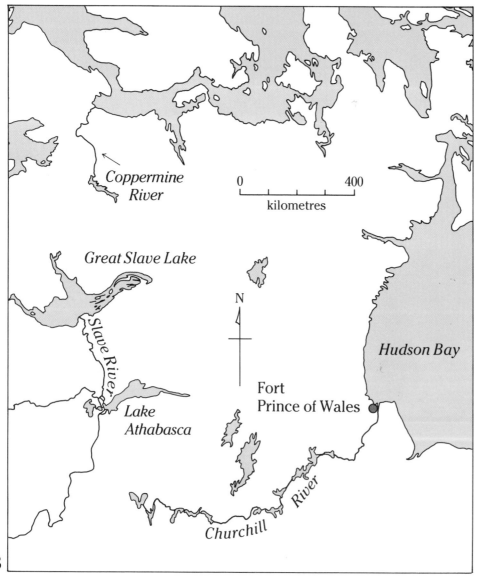

108

Matonabbee's Story

Our path took us through the forest. In many places we had to cut down trees to get the toboggans through. When the thaw began, we had a wind storm that lasted for three days. That wind was so strong you couldn't stand up in the open. We had to stay in the woods, in the shelter of the trees. The wind blew down many of the trees. We were lucky no one was hurt.

We had some good hunting. I remember we chased some moose over the hard snow until they couldn't run any more. Sometimes they would keep running for a whole day before they got tired and had to stop. Then we would kill them with a knife lashed to a long stick. Those moose wouldn't let you get too close to them.

Hearne and the Chipewyans are walking through a wind storm. Why would the wind make travelling more difficult?

One day we saw swans flying overhead on their way to the Barren Grounds. The snow was melting, and we could see the ground in many places. We stopped to make canoes because the ice had gone from the rivers and lakes. Spring had come.

Then we followed the caribou out of the forest onto the Barren Grounds. On we went towards the east. We killed caribou as we walked. We hung the meat on our packs to dry in the sun.

At last we came to a river that was a two-day walk from the fort. The wind was strong, and big waves filled the river. We had to stop because we could not cross it in our small canoes. At last the waves calmed down. Then we put our canoes in the river and paddled to the other side. We spent the night there, not far from the fort. The next morning we rose with the sun, took up our packs and marched on to Fort Prince of Wales.

That is the story of how I went to the copper mine with Samuel Hearne. It had been a long journey, with many hardships. I have to say that Hearne never got discouraged. He was a brave man, a fine traveller and a good friend.

How did Matonabbee show that he was also a brave man, a fine traveller and a good friend?

What Happened to Matonabbee?

Matonabbee became chief of all the Chipewyan Indians. He continued to travel across the Barren Grounds, bringing furs back to Fort Prince of Wales to trade. Matonabbee died in 1782. Hearne wrote that the death of this fine, intelligent man was a great loss.

What Happened to Samuel Hearne?

Samuel Hearne continued to work for the Hudson's Bay Company. In 1774 he journeyed up the Saskatchewan River and built a trading post called Cumberland House. It was the first building constructed by Europeans in what is now the province of Saskatchewan. Hearne became the **governor** of Fort Prince of Wales in 1776.

Later on, Samuel Hearne became ill and went back to England. His journey to the Coppermine River had made him famous. He decided to publish a journal of his travels. Samuel Hearne died in 1792, just before the book was published.

Hearne and Matonabbee have arrived at Fort Prince of Wales. How do you think the explorers might be feeling?

What Have We Learned?

Hearne went across the Barren Grounds to find a copper mine. He wanted to find out if ships from the Hudson's Bay Company could travel up the Coppermine River to the mine. Hearne was also looking for the Northwest Passage.

After many months of travel, Hearne reached the mine. When he got there, he found that there was very little copper in it. He also discovered that ships would never be able to travel up the Coppermine River. Most important, Hearne found that there was no Northwest Passage from Hudson Bay to the Pacific Ocean.

Hearne could not have survived on his journey without the help of the Indians. Matonabbee knew the way to the Arctic coast. He and the other Chipewyans knew how to make canoes for crossing the lakes and rivers on the way. They knew how to hunt caribou and buffalo for their food. The Chipewyans made Hearne warm clothes for the winter and cooked his food. Without the Chipewyan men and women, Hearne would have starved or frozen to death.

Hearne added a vast region to the map of Canada. He was the first European to stand on the northern coast of Canada. He was also the first European to see Great Slave Lake. Hearne was also the first person to map the Barren Grounds.

Hearne started out on his first journey onto the Barren Grounds in 1769 and returned from his third journey in 1772.

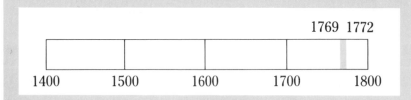

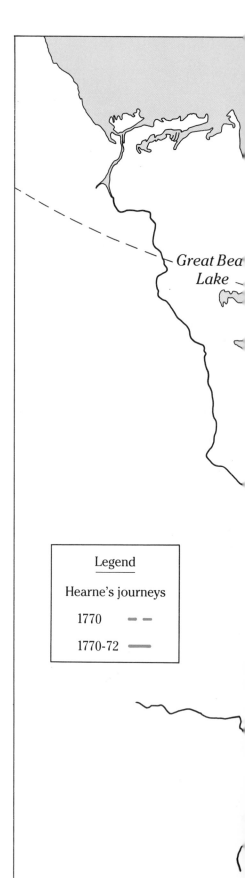

Great Bea[r]
Lake

Legend

Hearne's journeys

1770   ---

1770-72 ———

This map shows the routes of Hearne's second and third journeys. On which journey did he travel north of the Arctic Circle?

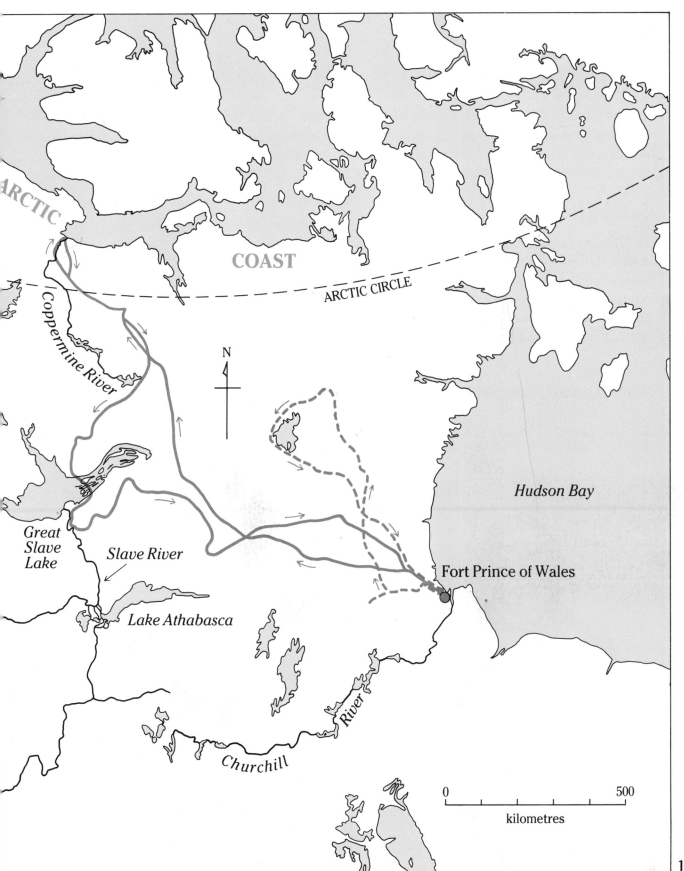

ARCTIC

COAST

ARCTIC CIRCLE

Coppermine River

N

Hudson Bay

Great
Slave
Lake

Slave River

Fort Prince of Wales

Lake Athabasca

Churchill River

0   500
kilometres

Two Points of View

Samuel Hearne called the large treeless region in northern Canada the Barren Grounds. Some people think that this is a good name for the region. The word *barren* means unproductive or bare. Others think that tundra is a better name. *Tundra* means treeless plains. The region has no trees, but it isn't completely barren.

Samuel Hearne

The region I travelled through was bare and empty. I saw nothing but rock, gravel, marshes and rivers. There are no trees, just moss growing on the rocky hills. The soil is thin. Farmers could not grow crops here. The climate is cold. Sometimes it even snows during the summer months. I call this harsh, unproductive region the Barren Grounds.

Why did Hearne call this area the Barren Grounds?
What did he have to compare it with?

Masak, an Inuit Woman

I live in the region where Hearne travelled. The tundra is full of life. Hundreds of different kinds of lichens and mosses grow here. Beautiful wildflowers bloom during the summer. Many birds, animals and fish live here. It is not easy to live or travel on the tundra, but it isn't empty or barren.

Why did Masak say that the area is not barren?
What did she have to compare it with?

114

Looking Back

Hearne's Three Journeys

Match the journeys in the first list with the events in the second list.

Journeys	Events
a. Hearne's first journey b. Hearne's second journey c. Hearne's third journey	1. Hearne's quadrant fell and broke. 2. Hearne saw Great Slave Lake. 3. Hearne found some copper. 4. Hearne left Fort Prince of Wales with a group of Indian men. 5. Hearne reached the Arctic coast. 6. The Indians left Hearne and went back to their homes.

How the Indians Helped

Look back through the chapter and find the different ways that Matonabbee and the other Chipewyans helped Hearne. Make a list of all the ways they helped.

Geography of the Barren Grounds

Hearne travelled through the part of the Canadian Shield called the Barren Grounds. Why was it so hard to explore the Barren Grounds? Give as many reasons as you can think of.

Imagine You Were There

What would you have said or done —
   if you were a Chipewyan and Hearne asked you to take him to the Coppermine River?
   if you were on the Barren Grounds in winter and could not find any caribou?
   if you had been with Hearne when he reached the Arctic coast?

Find Out More

1. While he was travelling across the Barren Grounds, Hearne met some Copper Indians. Use your library to find out something about this Indian group. Write a paragraph about the Copper Indians.
2. Find out what important minerals are mined in the Canadian Shield today. List the three most important minerals. After each mineral, write down some of the things it is used for.
3. Go to the library and find out more about Hearne. Make a list of the new things you have learned.

5

Who Explored the Pacific Coast?

What Lies Ahead?

In this chapter, you will find out the answers to these questions.

- What was the story of Juan de Fuca?

- Who was Captain Cook?

- What was Cook looking for and what did he find?

- Who was George Vancouver?

- What was Vancouver looking for?

- How did the Indians help Vancouver?

- What new things did Vancouver find out about the Pacific Coast?

This map shows the Pacific Coast of North America. What do you notice about the coastline?

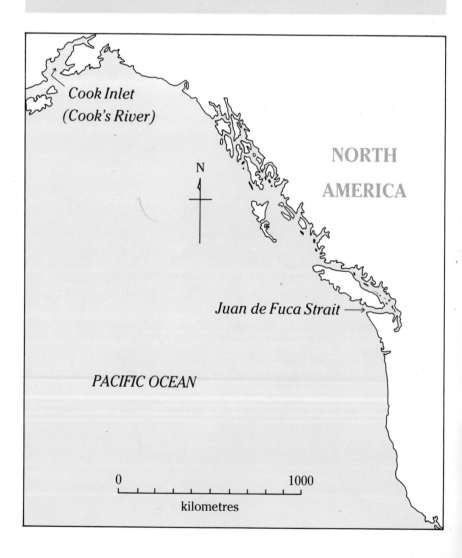

Cook Inlet
(Cook's River)

N

NORTH

AMERICA

Juan de Fuca Strait →

PACIFIC OCEAN

0   1000

kilometres

Early Explorers along the Pacific Coast

Samuel Hearne had travelled across the Barren Grounds to the Arctic coast. He had not found the Northwest Passage. Next, Europeans began to explore the Pacific Coast of North America. They thought they might find an entrance to the Northwest Passage there.

The Story of Juan de Fuca

A Greek sailor called Juan de Fuca said he had sailed along the Pacific Coast of North America in 1592. Far to the north he found a **strait**. De Fuca said he sailed through the strait to an inland sea. He thought the sea might lead to the Northwest Passage.

De Fuca said the land along the strait was rich in gold, silver and pearls. He also said he saw people dressed in animal skins.

No one knows for sure whether Juan de Fuca found a strait. The important thing is that explorers began looking for the Juan de Fuca Strait.

Do you think the story of Juan de Fuca is true? Why or why not?

Captain Cook Looks for the Northwest Passage

Captain James Cook was a famous English explorer. He made three long voyages from England to the Pacific Ocean.

In 1776 Captain Cook set out to look for the Juan de Fuca Strait. Although he did not find it, he kept sailing north. He hoped he would find the Northwest Passage.

One day Cook's ships entered a large **inlet**. Trees were floating in the water. Captain Cook thought the trees must have come down a very big river. He thought that such a big river might be the Northwest Passage. This river was put onto maps and called Cook's River.

Why did Captain Cook think the inlet he found might lead to the Northwest Passage?

Captain Cook was an English explorer. What kind of person do you think he was?

Who Was George Vancouver?

George Vancouver was born in England in 1757. He joined the British Navy when he was 14. When Vancouver was 15, he sailed with Captain Cook. Later Vancouver sailed to the Caribbean. By the time Vancouver set out to explore the Pacific Coast of North America, he was an experienced sailor.

George Vancouver Charts the Pacific Coast

One of the men who went with Captain Cook to look for the Northwest Passage was George Vancouver. In 1790, the British government asked Vancouver to explore the coast of northwest America. At this time the whole of northwest America was known as New Albion.

Vancouver's First Voyage

Vancouver was in charge of the voyage. He was given two ships, the *Discovery* and the *Chatham*. They were not very big. The *Discovery* had a crew of 100, and the *Chatham* had 45. Vancouver was commander of the *Discovery*, and William Broughton was commander of the *Chatham*.

The *Discovery* and the *Chatham* left England in 1791 and sailed south to the tip of Africa. From there they crossed the Indian Ocean and then sailed into the Pacific Ocean. The ships stopped for a while in the Sandwich Islands. Today they are called the Hawaiian Islands. Then the ships continued sailing northeast. At last, in April 1792, Vancouver and his men saw land. They had reached the west coast of North America. It had been over a year since they left England.

The Discovery *took this route from England to North America. Can you see why it took more than a year to get there?*

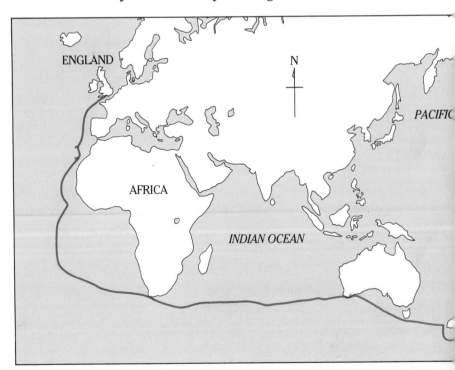

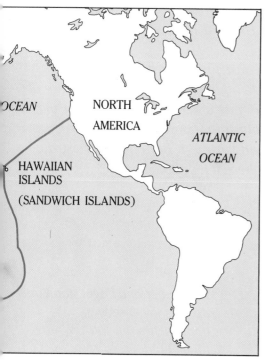

Above: Vancouver and his men are exploring the Pacific Coast. What do you think the sailors in the boat are doing?

OCEAN

NORTH
AMERICA

*ATLANTIC
OCEAN*

HAWAIIAN
ISLANDS

(SANDWICH ISLANDS)

Who Was Peter Puget?

Peter Puget was born in England in 1765. He went into the British Navy when he was 12. While Puget was serving in the Caribbean he met George Vancouver. The two men became friends. When Vancouver was asked to explore the northwest coast of America, he invited Peter Puget to go with him.

One of the officers on the *Discovery* was Peter Puget. We can pretend that Puget kept a diary of his journey to the region he called New Albion. Let us take a look at his diary and find out what happened to Peter Puget on his voyage with Vancouver.

Peter Puget's Diary
Sunday, April 29, 1792

It is hard to believe, but we have found Juan de Fuca's strait. When we left the Sandwich Islands, we headed northeast towards the coast of New Albion. Along the way we saw lots of whales jumping in the water. In one spot the ocean was covered with jellyfish as far as we could see. As we got closer to land, we saw ducks and puffins.

At last we sighted the coast of New Albion. We sailed northward along the coast. The weather was foggy, so it was difficult to find our latitude.

Then this morning we saw a remarkable sight. In the east rose the highest mountain we have seen. It was divided into two peaks and covered with snow. Another explorer had already named it Mount Olympus.

We also saw another ship this morning, the first we have seen in eight months. It was an American ship, commanded by Captain Robert Gray. Captain Vancouver sent me to talk to him. Captain Gray told me that we were only a short distance from Juan de Fuca's strait. He said he had entered the strait himself three years ago.

We continued along the coast to the north. It was not very long before we spotted a wide body of water. There we were at Juan de Fuca's strait. It was just where de Fuca said it was. Every man in the crews of both ships came on deck to look.

At the moment we are sailing through Juan de Fuca's strait. I can hardly wait to find out where it will take us.

What did the explorers hope to find at the end of Juan de Fuca's strait?

Vancouver and Puget stand on deck as the Discovery *approaches the coast. What is Puget holding?*

The *Discovery* and the *Chatham* were sailing through a strait like the one Juan de Fuca had described. Along the strait there were beaches of sand and rocks. Beyond the beaches lay a great forest of cedars and firs.

Vancouver was looking for a good **harbour**. When he found one, the ships were anchored and a camp was set up on shore. Then small boats were lowered from the ships and the men went off to map the coast. Each boat went in a different direction. The officer in charge of each boat had to make careful

A boat is being lowered from the Discovery. *Why were small boats used for mapping the coast instead of the large ships?*

notes and maps of the coast he was exploring. Sometimes a boat would be gone for two or three weeks.

About 8 km east of their harbour, the explorers found an inland sea. Vancouver sent Peter Puget out in a boat with some other men to explore the southern part of the sea. Today that part is called Puget Sound. Puget and his men were not the first Europeans to explore the **sound**. Some Spanish explorers had already been there. Puget and his men were the first to chart the sound completely.

What would the crew need to take in each small boat?

Peter Puget's Diary
Friday, June 1, 1792

For the first time in many weeks I am lying in my bunk on the Discovery. I have just returned from exploring the shores and islands of an inland sea. Captain Vancouver has named the south end of this inland sea after me—Puget Sound. I am proud that my name will be on the map.

Puget Sound is beautiful. It is filled with islands, large and small. We have a mast we can put up in our small boat. When a breeze springs up, we can raise the sail and sit back and watch the islands and bays pass by.

The land close to the water is quite flat. Most of it is covered with forest. In places there are open meadows. We saw many gooseberry, raspberry and currant bushes. Roses were blooming everywhere.

We saw several groups of Indians in Puget Sound. One day we were sitting on the beach eating our midday meal when eight Indian canoes paddled up to the shore. The Indians didn't know who we were or why we were there. They got out of their canoes and began to sharpen their arrows and spears on stones. I told the gunner to put a big charge of gunpowder into our little swivel gun and fire it. It was like fireworks, with a lot of smoke and noise. When the Indians heard the noise and saw all the smoke, they put their arrows and spears away. After that we traded buttons, knives and beads for their bows and arrows. In the end everything went off well. Towards evening the Indians went home, and we made camp for the night on shore.

How do you think the Indians felt when they saw Puget and the other men sitting on the shore?

This is a picture of the Discovery. *Would you like to have been on the* Discovery *with Vancouver?*

Vancouver and Puget then charted the northern part of the inland sea. Vancouver gave names to all the places he charted. Many were named after important people in England. The northern part of the inland sea was named the Strait of Georgia after King George. Some places were named after men on the two ships. Puget Sound was one. Others were named after Vancouver's friends and family. Vancouver named Sarah Point after his sister. Still other places were given names of plants. Vancouver saw berries at Strawberry Bay. Most of the names he chose are still used today.

After the inland sea had been charted, the ships continued north. Vancouver and his men kept charting the coast. By August they had reached Queen Charlotte Strait.

Vancouver charted this area in 1792. Can you find the places that he named?

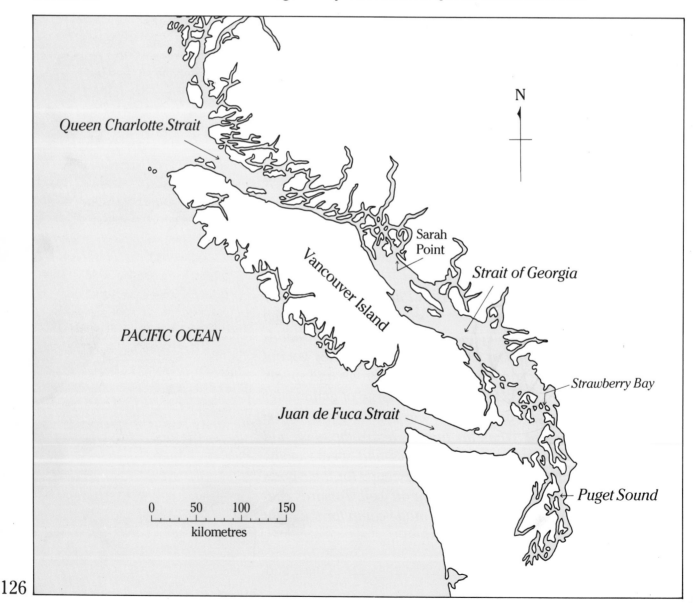

Peter Puget's Diary
Monday, August 6, 1792

Charting the coast is slow work. Many of the inlets are long. It takes the boats a long time to get around them. Wherever we look, we see giant trees.

It is exciting to explore so many new places. But it is also dangerous. We found that out today.

As we got farther up the Strait of Georgia, the islands got closer together. It was like going through a maze. There were so many islands we could hardly get through them.

At last we entered a wide body of water. We sailed into a **channel***. It was very foggy and there was not much wind. We were moving slowly through the water. Then disaster struck. Suddenly the* Discovery *jerked to a halt on a bed of hidden rocks. Captain Vancouver turned to me and said, "We're aground, Mr. Puget."*

Nobody was to blame. We were sailing in uncharted waters. The **tide** *was going out. Every second of every hour we risked hitting hidden rocks. We had been lucky until now.*

How might charting the Pacific Coast help sailors?

The coast of British Columbia is very dangerous. Often fog lies close to the water and sailors cannot see where they are going. Today many aids to **navigation** are used. Even so, ships sometimes hit rocks hidden below the water.

What Are the Ocean Tides?

The ocean is never still. It is always moving. The tides are one way the ocean moves. If you have ever been to the seashore, perhaps you have noticed that sometimes a large part of the beach is covered with water. Rocks may also be covered with water. This is high tide. At other times, you have to walk a long way out on the beach to get to the water. This is low tide. High tide and low tide each occur about twice a day.

Many animals and plants live in tide pools. These small pools are covered by the ocean at high tide and uncovered at low tide. In the picture you can see starfish and barnacles at low tide.

Peter Puget's Diary
Tuesday, August 7, 1792

Yesterday Captain Vancouver proved that he is a great leader. First he told us to take the anchor out of the Discovery. Then he told us to take down the top masts and let them float on the water. Next we started taking other things out of the ship to lighten it.

The tide was going out fast. I thought the Discovery was finished. She slowly heeled over until she was lying on her side like a beached whale. Her bow was way up out of the water. She was so far over on her side that the water was almost level with the deck.

Hours passed. Still we worked at taking things out of the ship. At last the tide turned. We watched the water slowly creep back over the rocks. The moment of crisis had come. Would the Discovery be able to right herself?

Then we saw the rigging on the lower masts tremble. The masts began to move. Slowly the Discovery began to right herself. When she was nearly upright, we pulled her free of the rocks with the stern line. Then, for the first time in many hours, I saw Captain Vancouver smile.

What do you suppose Vancouver was thinking during the hours the *Discovery* was grounded?

Vancouver continued to sail north of Vancouver Island. The men charted the coastline. By August 19, Vancouver had finished exploring for that year.

Then the *Discovery* and the *Chatham* sailed back to the Hawaiian Islands. There they met a supply ship. During the winter the ships were repaired. Charts were drawn of the Pacific Coast.

The Discovery *is aground. What will happen when the tide turns?*

PACIFIC COAST

The Pacific Coast

The Pacific Coast is a narrow region. It includes the Coast Mountains on the mainland and the islands off the coast. Vancouver charted the entire coastline. The pictures show you what the region looks like today.

The Coast Mountains are high and jagged. They were formed long ago by great forces within the earth. Later, the earth's climate became very cold. Great rivers of ice slowly moved over the land. Most of Canada became covered with ice called glaciers. On the

Left: People enjoy skiing in the Coast Mountains. You can see how high and jagged the peaks are.

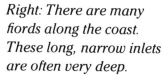

Right: There are many fiords along the coast. These long, narrow inlets are often very deep.

130

Pacific Coast, glaciers carved deep valleys. When the glaciers began to melt, the sea flowed into the valleys. These drowned valleys are called **fiords**. Vancouver explored many deep fiords along the coast.

Vancouver also saw vast coniferous forests. The Pacific Coast gets lots of rain, so trees grow very tall. Many ferns and mosses also grow in the wet forests.

The mountains, islands and fiords have not changed much since the *Discovery* sailed along the coast. If you sailed there today, you would still see many forests. The trees are used to make lumber and paper. Many people work in sawmills and paper mills.

The southern part of the Pacific Coast has changed the most. Many people live there. It is easier to build homes and farms on the flatter land. The largest city in the region is named after Captain Vancouver.

Above: You often see tugboats and log booms in this region.

Left: The coast forest is thick with trees, ferns and bushes.

131

Vancouver's Second Voyage

In the spring of 1793, the two ships sailed back to the coast of North America to start exploring again. They would begin to chart the coast where they had left off the year before. They would also continue to look for the Northwest Passage. The commander of the *Chatham*, William Broughton, had gone back to England. Peter Puget had been given command of the ship.

Do you think Peter Puget would be a good commander of the *Chatham*? Why or why not?

Peter Puget's Diary
Thursday, July 18, 1793

Well, I have been commander of the Chatham *for six months now. That means I have to work harder than ever to make sure nothing goes wrong.*

Exploring this coast is difficult. The weather is often foggy and rainy. We explore deep inlets that are filled with rocks. We still have not found the Northwest Passage.

I can't count the islands we have circled. There must be hundreds. Farther off the coast are the large Queen Charlotte Islands. We are not going to chart them. Our task is to chart the coastline.

We have had one bad experience. One day Mr. Johnstone, who is the sailing master on the Chatham, *and the men from his boat were eating breakfast in a cove. A few of the men found some mussels and ate them. Soon afterwards they got sick. The whole bodies became numb. One of the men died. Mr. Johnstone and the other men buried him at a bay where they stopped for the night. Captain Vancouver named it Carter's Bay in honour of the man who died.*

Slowly Vancouver and his men were charting the Pacific Coast. There were many deep fiords to explore. Sometimes they met Indians who lived along the fiords. Let's look in Peter Puget's diary and see what he says about meeting some Tlingit Indians.

These are some of the islands off the coast of British Columbia. Why would islands make exploring difficult?

Peter Puget's Diary
Wednesday, September 4, 1793

There's no wind today, so we can't sail along the coast. That gives me time to write about an interesting meeting we had with some Indians who live around here.

A few days ago the lookout shouted that three canoes were heading towards us. The canoes circled the ships while the Indians in them sang and slapped the water with their paddles. After that, two chiefs came on board the Discovery. *I hurried over from the* Chatham *to see them.*

The chiefs gave Captain Vancouver a sea otter skin and said they wished to trade. They had many fine salmon, and Captain Vancouver got enough for every man on both ships. Then Captain Vancouver took the chiefs down to the cabin and gave them some bread with molasses. The chiefs really liked it. In return, they gave us some whale oil. I know that the Indians here think whale oil is a treat, so I tried to swallow it with a smile. But I didn't really enjoy it very much.

Indian canoes approach the Discovery. How are these canoes different from those of other Indian groups you have learned about?

A little while later we were visited by another chief, the great Ononnistoy. He decided to spend the night on board the Discovery. When it got dark, we set off some fireworks in his honour.

The next morning Ononnistoy returned to the shore. He joined the other Indians where they had camped for the night. Then he and the other chiefs got into a large canoe and came alongside the Discovery. They sang some songs and presented Captain Vancouver with another sea otter skin. Then all the Indians came on board and the trading began. We gave the Indians blue cloth, tin kettles, spoons, looking glasses and beads. The Indians gave us masks, otter skins and fresh salmon. Everybody had a fine time. It reminded me of an English country fair, where people do a bit of trading and a lot of talking and laughing. I was sorry to see Ononnistoy and his

Vancouver and Ononnistoy begin trading. Why would Vancouver and his crew be glad to receive fresh salmon?

friends leave. For a few days they had made me feel at home in a country that is far from England.

Now I must get back to work. The wind is beginning to rise. Tomorrow we will sail north along the coast, exploring, drawing maps and looking for the Northwest Passage.

How were the customs of the Indians and the Englishmen the same? How were they different?

By the end of the summer Vancouver had finished exploring the northern part of the coast of what is now called British Columbia. On this voyage, Vancouver and his men had charted many inlets, bays and channels. Some of these were Burke Channel, Dean Channel and North Bentinck Arm. Again, Vancouver named every place he explored.

Above: Many sea otter used to live along the Pacific Coast. Why do you think there aren't very many sea otter left today?

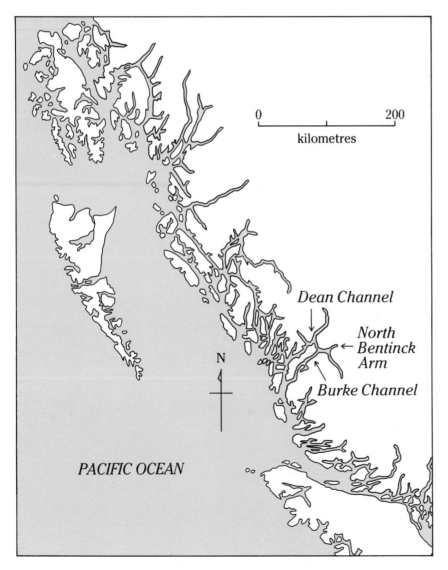

Vancouver charted this area in 1793. What is another name for the deep channels shown on the map?

How the Indians of the Northwest Coast Caught Salmon

Salmon was the main food of many Indians who lived along the Northwest Coast. Some of the Indians gave Vancouver and his men fresh salmon to eat. It tasted good and provided a healthful meal.

The Tlingit and the other tribes knew many ways to catch salmon. In rivers and streams, they often used harpoons. It was best to use harpoons in clear or shallow water. There the fisherman could see the fish. The fisherman stood in a canoe or on the bank to harpoon the fish.

Nets were also used to catch salmon. The Indians used dip nets to scoop salmon out of

The Northwest Coast Indians often used harpoons to catch salmon in rivers and streams.

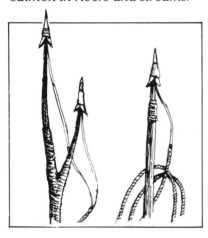

The Indians used many different types of nets to catch salmon.

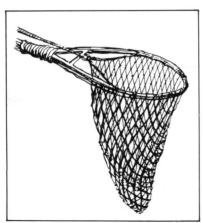

river traps. The Coast Salish Indians used large nets to catch salmon in the ocean. The net was hung between two canoes over a **reef**. The salmon would swim over the net. Then the fishermen would pull the net up into one of the canoes.

Weirs were often used to catch salmon. A weir is like a fence placed in a river or stream. The salmon could not get through the weir. The fishermen would spear the salmon or take them out of the water with a net. Sometimes openings in the weir led the salmon into a trap. Then the fishermen would use a net to take the salmon out of the trap.

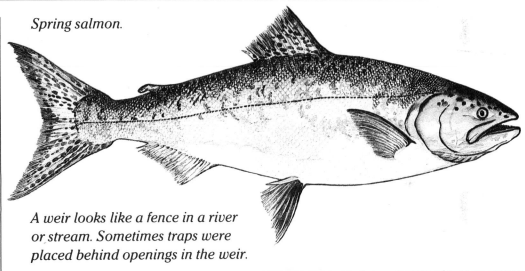

Spring salmon.

A weir looks like a fence in a river or stream. Sometimes traps were placed behind openings in the weir.

Vancouver's Third Voyage

As winter approached, the ships sailed back to the Hawaiian Islands. They waited there until spring. Then, in March 1794, the *Discovery* and the *Chatham* went back to the Pacific Coast of North America for the last time. It was Vancouver's last chance to find the Northwest Passage. This time he was going to look for Cook's River. He hoped it would lead to the Northwest Passage. Vancouver began his search along the Pacific Coast far to the north.

Peter Puget's Diary
Thursday, August 21, 1794

Tomorrow we sail for England. How can I describe all the things we have seen and done this year? In March we sailed back to New Albion to find Cook's River. On the way we ran into a fierce storm. For several days the temperature in my cabin was below freezing.

When we got to the river, Captain Vancouver told me to chart the lower part. Meanwhile, he would map the upper part.

What a job we had. The river was filled with big pieces of ice. Strong **currents** *pushed them back and forth. The bottom*

In 1794, Vancouver began charting the coast at Cook Inlet. He ended his work that year at Cape Decision. Can you find these two places on the map?

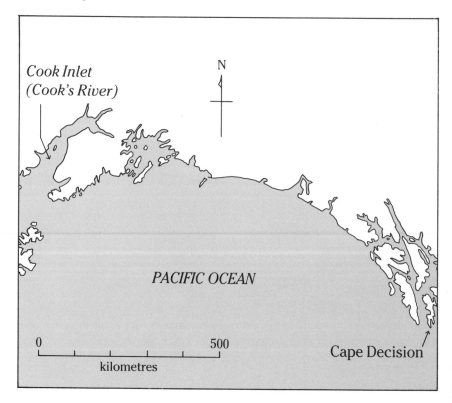

of the river was covered with rocks, making it dangerous to sail in shallow water.

When Captain Vancouver got to the end of the river, he found a wall of high mountains. Once again we were disappointed. Captain Cook had been mistaken. Cook's River was not a river. Captain Vancouver renamed it Cook Inlet.

Then we sailed southeast along the coast until we reached Cape Decision. That is where we stopped our survey last year. We didn't find the Northwest Passage after all. But we have mapped the whole coast of New Albion. We have named the islands, bays, straits and mountains.

I sit here in my tiny cabin on the Chatham *and wonder what the coast of New Albion will look like 200 years from now. Will people from Europe live here? I don't know. I just know it has been a great adventure to explore the coast of New Albion with Captain Vancouver.*

What would you like to tell Peter Puget about the Pacific Coast today?

The *Discovery* and the *Chatham* arrived in England in the fall of 1795. They had been gone four years and nine months. During that time Vancouver and his men had charted the Pacific Coast from the northern part of present-day California to the southern part of present-day Alaska. Their work was a remarkable achievement.

This is the head of Cook Inlet. Why was Vancouver disappointed when he saw the mountains?

What Happened to Peter Puget?

In 1797 Peter Puget became a captain in the British Navy. He fought in many battles at sea. Later Puget became commissioner of the navy in India, where he lived for several years. At last he became a rear admiral. During the final years of his life, Puget was ill. He died in 1822.

What Happened to George Vancouver?

When Vancouver got back to England, he was very ill. He left the navy and began writing a book about his voyages. He did not live to finish the book. George Vancouver died in 1798, at the age of 41. The important story of his explorations on the Pacific Coast of North America was finished by his brother, John Vancouver, and his friend, Peter Puget.

What Have We Learned?

Juan de Fuca said he had sailed up the Pacific Coast far to the north in 1592. He said he had found a strait that led to an inland sea. Explorers hoped that the Juan de Fuca Strait would lead to the Northwest Passage.

In 1776 Captain Cook sailed to the northwest coast of America to look for the Juan de Fuca Strait. He did not find it. He did find an inlet he thought was the entrance to a large river. Captain Cook thought the river might lead to the Northwest Passage. Mapmakers put this river on their maps and called it Cook's River.

In 1791 George Vancouver set out to explore the northwest coast of America. He was looking for the Northwest Passage. Over the next four and a half years, he made three voyages to the Pacific Coast.

Unlike most of the other European explorers who came to Canada, Vancouver did not depend very much on the Indians for help. Still, Vancouver and his men sometimes traded with the Indians they met. Often the Indians had fresh salmon, which they traded for cloth and metal.

On his first voyage, Vancouver sailed up the Juan de Fuca Strait. It did not lead to the Northwest Passage. On his second voyage, Vancouver finished exploring that part of the coast which is in present-day British Columbia. On his third voyage, Vancouver explored Cook's River. He found it was an inlet, not a river. He renamed it Cook Inlet. Vancouver discovered there was no entrance to the Northwest Passage along the Pacific Coast.

As they explored the coast, Vancouver and his men made careful notes and charts. Now mapmakers could make accurate maps of the Pacific Coast. Vancouver had added another region to the map of Canada.

In this chapter you have learned about exploration along the Pacific Coast from 1592 to 1794.

Page 143: This map shows the route Vancouver's ships took along the coast. Which part of the coast do you think was most difficult to chart?

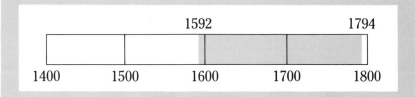

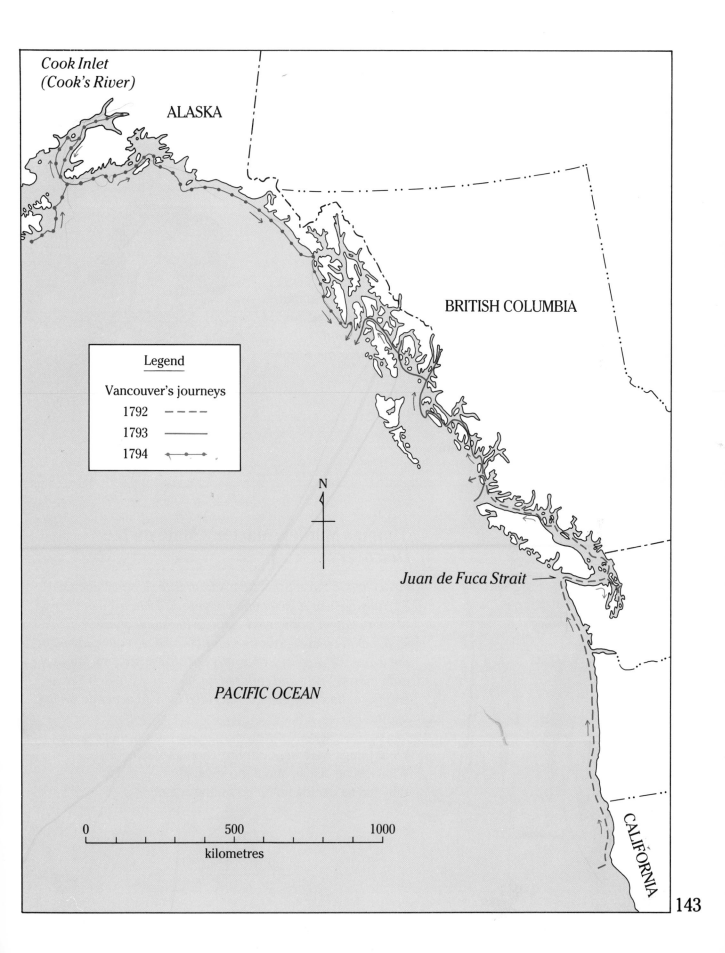

Cook Inlet
(Cook's River)

ALASKA

BRITISH COLUMBIA

Legend

Vancouver's journeys

1792

1793

1794

N

Juan de Fuca Strait

PACIFIC OCEAN

0   500   1000

kilometres

CALIFORNIA

143

Two Points of View

George Vancouver and his men saw many new places when they were charting the Pacific Coast. They were gone for four years. Some crew members thought the voyage was exciting. Others found it long and difficult.

James Johnstone, Master of the *Chatham*

I travelled to the coast of New Albion with George Vancouver. For me, the journey was exciting. I liked exploring new places. The mountains and fiords of New Albion are the most beautiful sights I have ever seen. I always hoped that we would find the Northwest Passage. My greatest thrill was when Captain Vancouver named one of the straits we mapped after me. I look forward to my next voyage.

What things were important to James Johnstone?
What did he like about the voyage?
Why did he want to go sailing again?

Thomas Manley, Master's Mate on the *Discovery*

I travelled to the coast of New Albion with George Vancouver. The voyage was difficult and dangerous. I was tired at the end of every day. It wasn't easy living in the small quarters of the ship. I didn't like the storms. Our little ship was often tossed by the waves for days at a time. Most of all, I missed my family. I didn't see my wife and children for over four years. When we finally got back to England, I decided I would never go sailing again.

What things were important to Thomas Manley?
What did he dislike about the voyage?
Why did he decide not to go sailing again?

Looking Back

Explorers and Their Achievements

Match the explorers in the first list with the achievements in the second list.

Explorers

a. Juan de Fuca
b. Captain James Cook
c. George Vancouver
d. Peter Puget

Achievements

1. I explored a large sound, which was later named after me.
2. I mapped the entire coast of New Albion.
3. I found a strait along the Pacific Coast.
4. I found a river I thought would lead to the Northwest Passage.
5. I named all the places I explored.

How the Indians Helped

The Indians who lived along the Pacific Coast gave Vancouver and his men fresh salmon to eat. Give reasons why trading for salmon might have helped Vancouver and his crew.

Geography of the Pacific Coast

Here is a list of place names that Vancouver chose. Which ones are bodies of water? Which ones are places on the land?

Sarah Point   Burke Channel
Puget Sound   North Bentinck Arm
Strait of Georgia   Cook Inlet
Strawberry Bay   Carter's Bay
Cypress Island   Cape Decision

Write definitions in your notebook for any two of the land forms and any two bodies of water.

Imagine You Were There

What would you have said or done —
   if Vancouver had asked you to go with him to explore the unknown coast of New Albion?
   if you had been on board the *Discovery* when it grounded?
   if you were a Tlingit Indian and you saw the *Discovery* and the *Chatham* sailing along

Find Out More

1. The Indian tribes who lived along the Pacific Coast told many interesting legends. Find some of these legends in the library and read them. Then make up a legend of your own.
2. Captain Cook made several important voyages. Go to the library and find out more about Captain Cook. Then write a paragraph about what you have learned.
3. The fiords along the Pacific Coast were formed long ago when glaciers began to melt. Find out more about glaciers. Write a paragraph about what you have learned.

6

Who Explored the Western Mountains?

Peter Pond Explores the Northwest

Peter Pond and some other fur traders are resting at an Indian camp. Why do you think they stayed with the Indians?

Anthony Henday had crossed the prairies and camped near the Rocky Mountains. Samuel Hearne had journeyed across the Barren Grounds to the Arctic coast. These explorers had not found the Northwest Passage. Other explorers continued

to move west across the continent. They went northwest into the forest. They hoped to find a river there that flowed to the Pacific Ocean.

Most of the Europeans who explored the northern forest were fur traders. One of these traders was Peter Pond. In 1777 Pond journeyed up the Churchill River until he came to a high ridge of land. Pond had reached the Methye Portage. When he got to the other side of the portage, he found that the rivers flowed north. Pond decided to follow one of the rivers. It led to the Lake of the Hills, which is called Lake Athabasca today. Later Pond journeyed farther north to Great Slave Lake.

Peter Pond opened up the Athabasca country for the fur trade. The winters in Athabasca were long and cold. As a result, the beavers there had very thick fur. Fur traders could get a lot of money for these furs. The only problem was that Athabasca was 4000 km away from Montreal. It took a very long time to get the furs back there. The rivers were dangerous and many furs were lost in the rapids. If the traders could find a river to the Pacific Ocean, then they could send their furs there. From there the furs could be sent to Europe by ship. That would save time and money.

Why did fur traders want to find a river to the Pacific Ocean?

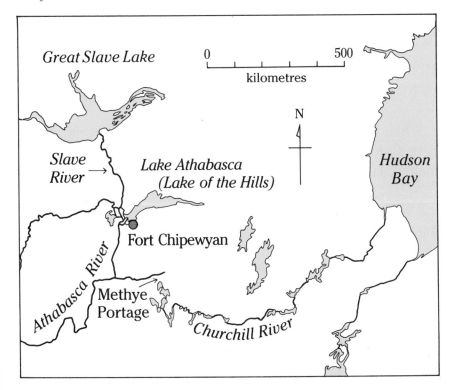

Peter Pond travelled from the Churchill River to Lake Athabasca. How is the Churchill River different from the Athabasca River?

149

Who Was Alexander Mackenzie?

Alexander Mackenzie was born in 1763 on the Isle of Lewis in Scotland. He came to Canada when he was 15 years old.

The next year he went to work for a fur trading company. By the time he was 20, he was a partner in the firm. Later this company joined others to form the North West Company.

In 1787 Mackenzie travelled to Fort Chipewyan. From this small trading post he set out on two great voyages of discovery. Mackenzie kept a journal of each of these voyages.

Mackenzie Searches for a River to the Pacific Ocean

In 1783–84 a new fur trading company was formed. It was called the North West Company. Peter Pond was a partner in the company. In 1787 the North West Company sent a young trader to the Athabasca country. His name was Alexander Mackenzie.

Mackenzie spent a winter with Pond at Fort Chipewyan. Pond told Mackenzie about his explorations. He showed Mackenzie a map he had drawn. His map showed a river flowing from Great Slave Lake to the Pacific Ocean. Mackenzie decided he would try to find this river flowing west.

Mackenzie's First Journey

In June of 1789 Mackenzie was ready to start on his first voyage. He did not go alone. He took four voyageurs with him to paddle his canoe. A Chipewyan Indian chief was in another canoe. Two other Indians were in a third canoe. The Indians would act as hunters and interpreters. Several Indian women went along as well. They would cook the food and mend the clothes. The final member of the crew was a German named John Steinbruck.

Would you like to have been part of Mackenzie's crew? How might you persuade him to take you along?

When it was time for the explorers to set out, everyone at Fort Chipewyan came to say goodbye. The canoes were loaded. The explorers waited for the order to leave.

At last the steersman lifted his pole. When he pushed it into the water, the voyageurs began to paddle. Off they went, singing a paddling song. The people who stayed behind at the fort shouted to the explorers. They wished them luck in their search for the river to the Pacific Ocean.

Let us pretend that John Steinbruck kept a diary of his journey with Mackenzie. If we look into Steinbruck's diary, we can find out what happened on the first part of the journey.

Who Was John Steinbruck?

No one knows who John Steinbruck was. Perhaps he came to Canada to learn about the fur trade. Maybe he met some North West Company traders who invited him to visit the Athabasca country. All we know is that Steinbruck was with Mackenzie on his first journey to find the Pacific Ocean.

FORT CHIPPEWAYAN

This drawing shows what Fort Chipewyan looked like during Mackenzie's time. Notice that the name of the fort was spelled differently then. What can you tell about the land around Fort Chipewyan from this drawing?

John Steinbruck's Diary
Friday, June 5, 1789

The great adventure of my life has begun. Two days ago we left Fort Chipewyan. Now we are going down the Slave River. The land along the river is low. It is covered with birch trees, pines and poplars.

Already I admire our leader, Alexander Mackenzie. He is young and has red hair. He also has a hot temper. When he is angry his blue eyes flare like a wind-driven fire. When I look at him I think of the Vikings.

Today was filled with excitement. We came to some rapids and a high waterfall. That meant we had to portage. Suddenly we heard a shout. One of the women was in a canoe that was going towards the waterfall. Luckily, she jumped out before the canoe reached the falls. We held our breath as she scrambled to shore. The canoe went down the falls and was dashed to pieces. The woman was lucky to be alive.

Now we are camped for the night. The hunters and the women provided us with a feast—seven geese, a beaver and four ducks. We are all tired, but at least we are not hungry.

Why did this meal seem like a feast to the explorers?

Mackenzie and his men worked a long day. They would start paddling at two or three in the morning and go on until five or six in the evening. Then they would camp and eat supper.

Mackenzie was in a hurry to reach Great Slave Lake. The hunters did not have time to leave the river and hunt for deer or moose. Instead, they shot swans, geese and ducks, which nested by the river.

When the explorers came to Great Slave Lake, it was covered with ice. Somehow Mackenzie had to find a way through the ice to the western end of the lake.

The Indian woman is jumping out of her canoe as it rushes towards the waterfall. Why do you think the woman stayed in her canoe so long?

John Steinbruck's Diary
Monday, June 29, 1789

We have had a terrible time crossing the lake. It was covered with great ice floes. We never knew when a change of wind might send one of the floes towards our canoes. We would set off, the voyageurs singing "En roulant ma boule" ("A-rolling my ball"). For a while all would be well. Then in the distance we would hear the ice floes grinding. When we heard that sound, we made for the nearest beach.

The beaches were not much better. Clouds of mosquitoes attacked us. They covered our hands and faces and the food we ate. Sometimes I ate more mosquitoes than meat.

*We stopped at an island in the lake and buried two bags of **pemmican**. That way we will be sure we have something to eat when we come back this way.*

A few days ago we met some Copper Indians. Mr. Mackenzie asked one of them to take us to the place where the river leaves the lake. The Indian had not been to that place for many years. He led us on a wild goose chase from bay to bay. After much searching, the Copper Indian finally brought us to the place where the river sweeps out of the lake.

What were some of the difficulties the explorers experienced as they crossed the lake?

The explorers are paddling through the ice floes on the lake. What might happen if they hit one of the ice floes?

How the Chipewyans Made Pemmican

The Indians made long journeys through the wilderness. Often it was hard to find food. For this reason, some tribes took pemmican with them. Pemmican was dried meat. It could last for years without spoiling. It could be eaten cold or cooked. A small amount could keep a person going for days.

Pemmican was made from a large animal. The Chipewyans used caribou meat. The Indians on the prairies made pemmican from buffalo meat.

Mackenzie took pemmican on his two long journeys. The explorers often buried pemmican along the way. Then they would be sure to have something to eat on the return journey.

Here is how the Indians made pemmican.

1. The meat was cut into thin slices.

2. The meat was then placed on a drying rack in the sun or over a fire to dry.

3. The dried meat was placed on a flat stone. Then it was pounded with another stone until it was almost a powder.

4. Next animal fat was melted. While it was still hot, the fat was mixed with the pounded meat. Sometimes berries were added as well.

5. The pemmican was put into skin bags or birch-bark baskets. As it cooled, it became hard. Then it was ready to carry.

Strips of meat to be used for pemmican are drying in the sun.

This woman is pounding strips of dried meat with a stone.

Sometimes pemmican was boiled over the fire to make a sort of stew.

157

Mackenzie had found a broad and swift river. Today it is called the Mackenzie River. The explorers were moving with the current and covered many kilometres each day. They saw lots of geese and ducks, which the hunters killed for food. Summers in the north are short. Mackenzie did not know how long the river was, so he pushed his crew members to their limit. The voyageurs did not complain. They, too, wanted to find out where the great river went.

John Steinbruck's Diary
Sunday, July 5, 1789

After we had found the river, Mr. Mackenzie was happy for a few days. He even sang along with the voyageurs. Now he is gloomy, and I can understand why. My **compass** *tells me that we are not going west. We are going north.*

Two days ago we camped at the foot of a high hill. Mr. Mackenzie suggested that we climb it. Up the hill we went with a voyageur and some Indians. It took an hour and a half to reach the top. In the distance we could see a range of low mountains. There were no trees except a few small pines and birches. Below us we could see a lot of small lakes. They were covered with white swans. I have never seen so many swans before in my life. It was a wonderful sight.

Today we met a group of Dogrib and Slave Indians. They had never seen people from Europe before. Mr. Mackenzie gave the Indians gifts: axes, knives, awls and beads. Later on, the Indians danced in our honour. Men and women formed a circle. They danced and sang, beating out the time with bone rattles.

The Indians' clothes are made from caribou skins. They are trimmed with coloured porcupine quills and pieces of fur. Even the little children and babies wear decorated clothes.

Mackenzie and the other explorers are giving gifts to the Slave and Dogrib Indians. Why did the explorers give gifts to the Indians?

Mr. Mackenzie asked the Indians about the river. They said the river led to the sea but that it would take us several winters to get there. The Indians said terrible rapids would wreck our canoes. We were unhappy to hear this. Still, Mr. Mackenzie has decided not to turn back until he sees where the river ends. I feel the same way. I want to be able to say I have been to the mouth of this river.

As the explorers paddled towards the north, they saw many cranes. What do you think the crane in this picture is doing?

As the explorers went on, the country became more and more barren. The only trees they saw were dwarf willows, which were as small as bushes. The ground was frozen solid below the surface. Yet there were birds everywhere: ducks, geese, swans and cranes.

The explorers were now north of the **Arctic Circle**. The Mackenzie River was taking them farther north. It was not flowing towards the Pacific Ocean.

What do you suppose Mackenzie was thinking as he paddled along the river?

John Steinbruck's Diary
Saturday, July 11, 1789

Last night Mr. Mackenzie and I sat up to watch the sun. It did not set. At midnight the sky was as bright as it is at midday.

Today we found an abandoned Eskimo camp. Around the burnt-out fires there were pieces of whalebone and leather. Our guide says we will soon reach a large lake where many Eskimos live. There we will see whales and large white bears. It sounds like a strange land.

I think back to the day when I landed in Montreal. How little I knew of this vast land and its people. How could I ever have imagined the flocks of birds that fill the sky? Or the herds of caribou that stretch to the horizon? I ask myself if people from Europe could ever live in this land. To live here, men and women must be heroic. They must be like the people who have journeyed with Mr. Mackenzie down this great river.

Mackenzie knew the river would not take him to the Pacific Ocean. He was disappointed. Still, he wanted to find out where the river would lead. After leaving the deserted Inuit camp, the voyageurs paddled on to the north. At last they came to the end of the river. They had reached the Arctic coast.

John Steinbruck's Diary
Wednesday, July 15, 1789

We are camped on an island in an ice-filled sea. At first we did not know it was the ocean. All we could see was ice. We camped on the beach, close to our canoes. We ate supper and talked and then lay down to sleep. Hours later, we were awakened by icy water lapping at our feet. Then we realized it was the ocean tide. We knew we had reached the end of the river at last. Mr. Mackenzie is very disappointed that this river has not carried us to the Pacific Ocean. He has named it the River of Disappointment.

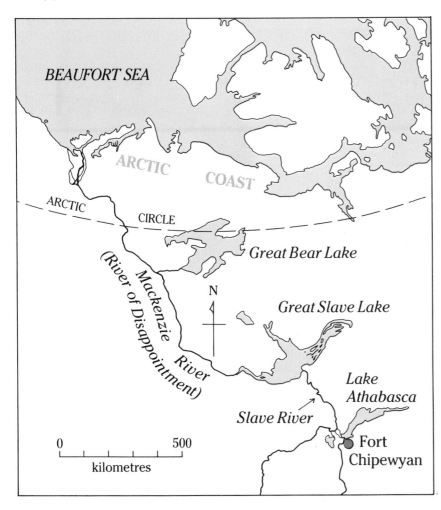

On his first journey, Mackenzie travelled along the Mackenzie River to the Arctic coast. At first the Mackenzie River flows west from Great Slave Lake. Then what happens?

Yesterday we saw some large animals in the water. At first we thought they were pieces of ice. Then we realized they were white whales. We chased them in our canoe, but we couldn't catch up to them.

We are at the end of our exploration, although it is not the end of our journey. We start back to Fort Chipewyan tomorrow. In a way, I am sorry we cannot go on exploring this immense country.

I have often been wet and cold. My feet and hands are a mass of cuts and bruises. Still, I am happy. The one regret I have is that I will not be with Mr. Mackenzie when he sets out again to find a path to the Pacific Ocean.

How did the explorers know they had reached the Arctic coast?

The explorers are chasing white whales. Would you like to chase whales in a canoe?

The journey back up the Mackenzie River was difficult. It took many weeks. Now the explorers were going **upstream** against the current. That meant they had to use poles to push the canoes along. Sometimes they were forced to wade in the

icy water, dragging the canoes. On the journey **downstream** they had often travelled 120 km a day. Going back, they were lucky to cover 40 km in 14 hours of poling and pulling.

At last Mackenzie and his crew reached Great Slave Lake. This time it was easy to cross, since all the ice had melted. They entered the Slave River. Within a few days they reached Lake Athabasca. Ahead lay Fort Chipewyan. Mackenzie and his men had been gone 102 days and had covered more than 3300 km. Now they were going home to rest.

Why was it harder travelling back to the fort than it had been travelling to the coast?

What Happened to John Steinbruck?

No one knows what happened to John Steinbruck. He is mentioned only once in Mackenzie's journal, at the beginning. We do not know what he did after the journey to the Arctic coast. Perhaps Steinbruck went back to Germany, married and had a family. Perhaps he sometimes sat by the fireside in the evening and told his children the story you have just read.

[Ma]ckenzie's Second Journey

[Alexa]nder Mackenzie was still determined to find the river [that fl]owed to the Pacific Ocean. He had to wait almost three [years b]efore he could search once again. During that time, he [spent a] year in England. He studied navigation there.

[Macke]nzie's plan was simple. He would go west along the [Peace Ri]ver. Then he would find a route through the Rocky [Mountain]s. Once he was over the Rockies, he believed he [would find] the great river to the Pacific Ocean.

[In the fa]ll of 1792 Mackenzie began his journey up the Peace River. He stopped at a spot close to where the town of Peace River stands today. There he built a fort and waited for the winter to pass.

..as part of
...ey!

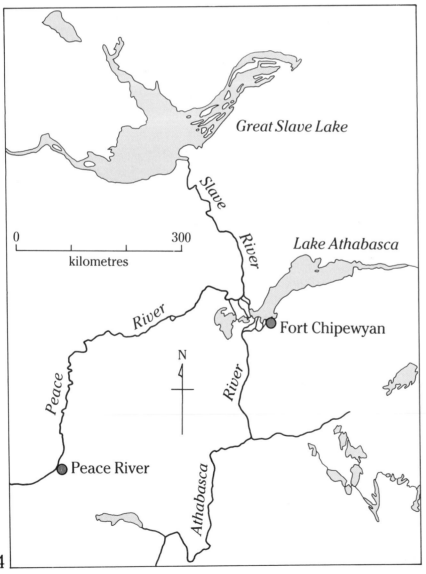

Why do you think Mackenzie travelled only part way up the Peace River?

In May Mackenzie and his crew set out. They travelled in one large canoe. With Mackenzie were six voyageurs, two Indian hunters and Mackenzie's assistant, Alexander Mackay. Mackenzie's dog went along, too. Mackenzie must have been pleased to have Mackay with him. Mackay had travelled a lot before. He was also easygoing and reliable.

We know that Mackenzie kept a journal of his great explorations. Did Mackay keep a diary, too? We can pretend that he did and that we have found it. Let's read it and find out what happened as Mackenzie searched for the river to the Pacific Ocean.

Who Was Alexander Mackay?

It is not known when Alexander Mackay was born. He joined the North West Company in 1791. Then he went to Fort Chipewyan to work with Alexander Mackenzie. One other interesting fact about Mackay is that his sister married Simon Fraser, who later explored the river that is now named after him.

Mackenzie began his second journey along the Peace River. What do you think it would be like to paddle along this part of the river?

Alexander Mackay's Diary
Sunday, May 19, 1793

When I made up my mind to keep a diary, I told myself I would write something in it every day. There just hasn't been enough time. Now, for the first time, I've got a chance to write about our journey so far.

*The first part of our journey was smooth going. We passed through wide meadows where herds of elk and buffalo were feeding. Then the land changed. We left the meadows and moved into the hills. Now we are in a **canyon**. It is narrow, and the water pours through with frightening speed. Because of the many rapids and waterfalls, we have to drag the canoe along from the shore. Stones keep rolling down from the cliffs above, so we are always in danger of being hit.*

Today Mr. Mackenzie, the Indians and I scouted ahead. Mr. Mackenzie's dog came with us. The canyon walls were so steep we had to move from tree to tree. One false step, one rotten branch, and we would have fallen into the rapids.

The voyageurs struggle on. Their faces are grim, and I wonder if they can take much more of this terrible struggle. Mr. Mackenzie won't think of turning back. He is determined to find a path through the mountains.

What was the job of the voyageurs? What might happen if they decided to turn back?

Mackenzie had no idea what he was getting into when he entered the Peace River Canyon. Perhaps that was just as well. If Mackenzie and his men had known what they were about to face, they might have turned back. Perhaps they would have looked for another way around that terrible stretch of water.

Mackenzie and his men kept struggling against the raging water that threatened to sweep them and their canoe away. At last the day came when they could go no farther. Ahead of them lay a stretch of churning white water. It was on this day that Mackenzie decided to portage over the mountain.

The explorers are struggling through the Peace River Canyon. Why aren't they paddling in their canoe?

The Cordillera

CORDILLERA

The Cordillera is a large **chain** of mountains and valleys. Mackenzie searched for a route through the mountains. The pictures show this region today.

Like the mountains on the Pacific Coast, the Cordillera was formed long ago. Later, glaciers carved out peaks and valleys. The mountains of the Cordillera are high and jagged.

Many rivers flow through the Cordillera. Mackenzie was looking for a river to take him to the Pacific Ocean. As he found out, some of these rivers are very steep and wild.

Left: People like to hike and camp in the Cordillera.

Right: Rafting is a popular sport on the rivers that flow through the Cordillera.

Below: In summer, the meadows above the tree line are filled with wildflowers.

If you followed Mackenzie's route, you would find three main areas. In the east there are several mountain ranges, including the Rockies. Travelling west, you would next reach a lower, flatter area. Then there are more mountains. These are the eastern slopes of the Coast Mountains. The western slopes are part of the Pacific Coast region.

The lower slopes of the mountains are covered with coniferous trees. Many trees are used for lumber. Skilled workers cut and take trees from the mountain slopes. Farther up the mountains, above the tree line, there are meadows. They are filled with wildflowers in summer. Even higher, it is too cold for any-thing to grow. The tops of the mountains are covered with snow.

The flatter region between the mountains is very dry. It is covered with grassland. Ranchers keep beef cattle here. In the south it is warm enough to grow fruit in some areas.

The Cordillera has not changed very much since Mackenzie explored it. Even today, there are not a lot of people living in this region. Most of them live in towns near jobs in forestry, farming or mining.

Above: Logging is important on the lower slopes of the mountains.

Left: There are many cattle ranches in the flatter area of the Cordillera.

Alexander Mackay's Diary
Wednesday, May 22, 1793

Today we cut a trail up the mountainside. We are going to portage the canoe and our goods to the top of the rapids. We can no longer drag the canoe upstream. The river is filled with rapids, and the canyon is too narrow.

We cut down trees to clear a path up the steep mountain. Then we tied a rope to the canoe and hauled it along the path. It was exhausting work. I know now why some people say Mr. Mackenzie works his men too hard. When we meet an obstacle, he won't rest until we're over it. Rapids, rocks and mountains won't stand in his way.

Mr. Mackenzie has an amazing effect on us. We look at rapids, shake our heads and say, "No, we can't get through that." Then along comes Mr. Mackenzie. He looks at the water and says, "That's nothing to worry about." And through it we go. He makes all obstacles seem smaller than they really are. How does he do it? Maybe he makes us feel we are twice as big and strong as we really are. That's why the voyageurs admire him. They respect people who have the strength and courage to try the impossible. They are like that themselves.

Well, we finally got to the top of the mountain. I don't know how we did it. We are resting here for a few hours. Tomorrow we start cutting a path down the other side of the mountain to the top of the rapids.

What is Mackay's opinion of Mackenzie?

Mackenzie and the other explorers are hauling the canoe up the mountainside. Why did they have to cut down trees?

After Mackenzie and his men reached the top of the rapids, they could paddle their canoes once again. At last the explorers reached a **fork** in the Peace River. There the river divided into two rivers.

Mackenzie remembered what an old Indian hunter had told him. In order to pass through the mountains, Mackenzie must follow the river on the left-hand side. The voyageurs wanted to go up the river on the right-hand side. That river was wider and smoother. Mackenzie said they must follow the old hunter's advice, so they went along the river on the left. Today it is called the Parsnip River.

In many places the river was so swift the voyageurs could not paddle the canoe. Instead they pulled themselves along by the branches of trees. Day after day they struggled on. They were so tired they could travel no more than a few kilometres each day.

Do you think Mackenzie was right to follow the Indian's advice? Why or why not?

At the fork in the Peace River, Mackenzie went left onto the Parsnip River. What is the name of the other river he could have taken?

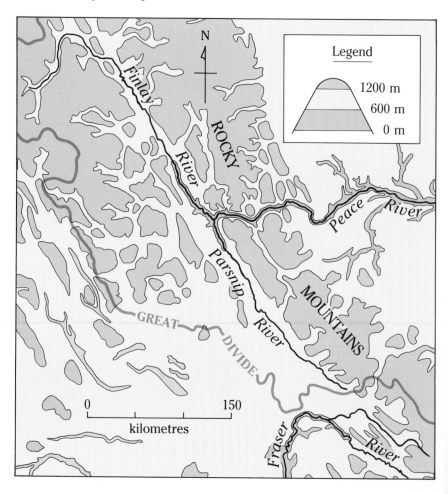

Alexander Mackay's Diary
Tuesday, June 11, 1793

I've done it again. Almost three weeks have passed since I last wrote in my diary. What a time we have had. The farther we went along the river, the more the mountains closed in on us. I am used to travelling in the wilderness, but I have never felt so lost as during these past few days. No matter where I looked, all I could see was a sea of mountains.

Then, without warning, we came upon a small band of Indians. At first they were frightened and ran off. Our hunters shouted that we came as friends. The Indians then came back out of the forest. Mr. Mackenzie gave them beads and pemmican. These gifts sealed our friendship.

Mr. Mackenzie asked the Indians if they knew of a river leading to the Western Ocean. One of the men said there was a great river that went towards the midday sun. He said he would take us to a stream that led to the river.

The little stream we entered was very narrow. We could hardly get the canoe along it. At last we came to a small lake, shaped like a finger. I glanced at Mr. Mackenzie's face. He was staring at a ridge of land. He gripped my arm. I could feel his hand shaking with excitement. "Look, Alex, look," he said. "We've done it. We've reached the place where the waters divide."

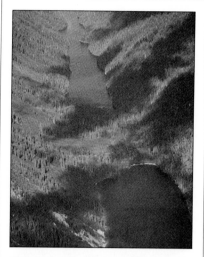

What Is the Great Divide?

The Great Divide is an area of very high land in the mountains. It follows the highest ridges. It is called a **divide** because the water that falls upon it flows in different directions. Rivers on the east side of the divide flow to the Arctic Ocean or to Hudson Bay. Rivers on the west side flow to the Pacific Ocean.

The Sekani Indians had shown the explorers how to reach the Great Divide. Now Mackenzie knew for sure he could get through the Rocky Mountains. He could follow the rivers flowing to the Pacific Ocean.

The canoe has hit some rocks and is splitting open. What would you do if you were in the canoe?

174

Alexander Mackay's Diary
Thursday, June 13, 1793

Yesterday we triumphed. We crossed over the ridge that divides the water. There are two small lakes, one on each side of the divide. We counted the paces over the divide from one lake to the other. There are 817. We stood at the very peak of the land and watched as water came down the mountain on one side and flowed into one lake. Then, just a few paces away, the water came down on the other side and flowed into the other lake. We all drank a toast to celebrate crossing the divide.

Well, that was yesterday. Today ended in calamity. We had travelled through three lakes and were in a fast-flowing river. Suddenly the canoe hit a rock and was flung sideways. One of the voyageurs caught hold of a branch, hoping to stop us. Instead, we rushed on, and he was flung from the canoe. Luckily, he landed on the shore and was not hurt. Then the canoe hit several rocks. The force of the water and the rocks split it wide open. Somehow we held onto the flattened canoe and dragged it to shore. We stood there shivering and staring at our wrecked canoe while the dog ran around barking and shaking water from its coat.

I believe we would still be standing there if Mr. Mackenzie hadn't told us to get the baggage off the wrecked canoe. Then he told us to build a fire, and we cooked a great pot of food. After we had eaten and our clothes were dry, Mr. Mackenzie spoke to us. This is what he said.

When you asked to join me in this voyage, I told you there would be danger. I told you there would be hardship. I said there would be risk to life and limb. I did not force anyone to come with me. You asked to come. Why? Because you wanted to stand with me on the shores of the Pacific. You wanted to cross over the western mountains. You are North West Company men. You are Canadian voyageurs, men of honour and men of courage. Will you turn back now because of a small accident? No, I don't think so. Our canoe will be mended. If we cannot mend it, then we will build another. We will go on. We will go on until we are standing on the shores of the Pacific Ocean.

When Mr. Mackenzie had finished speaking, we stood and cheered him. All of us promised to go with him until we reached the sea.

Why do you think the explorers promised to continue their journey?

The next day the explorers patched up the canoe. On June 15, they set off again. Going down the shallow, rapid river was a nightmare. Often the explorers had to clear a path through the thick woods and carry the canoe. Because of all the patches, the canoe was very heavy. Some days Mackenzie and his crew travelled only a few kilometres.

At last they entered a wide river. Today it is called the Fraser River. Mackenzie thought he had found the great river that would take him to the Pacific Ocean.

Mackenzie and his crew entered the Fraser River. What was the land like along the river?

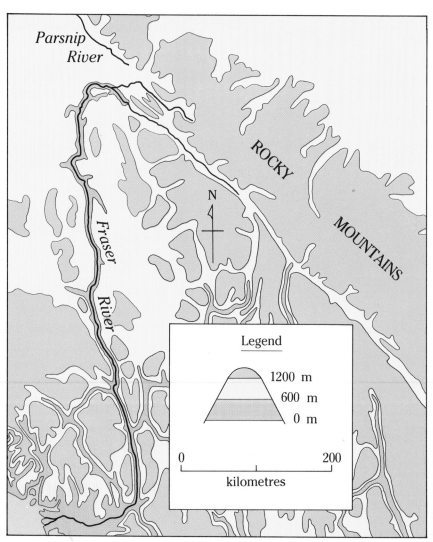

Alexander Mackay's Diary
Monday, June 24, 1793

We had a terrible time getting our heavy canoe through the thick woods and the mud to the river. We almost lost Mr. Mackenzie's dog. One of the Indians and I were scouting ahead to see if we could find the great river. When we got to the lower part of the river, we found that it was full of fallen wood. The dog was following us. He went running over the wood and fell into the water. The current was so strong it carried him under the wood. Luckily, we managed to get him out.

We have been following a large river south for many days. Now we are leaving it. Mr. Mackenzie has decided to march west on an Indian trail. His reasons are good. The Indians we have met say that this river is very long and filled with rapids. It will take a long time to get to the end of the river, and we don't have much time to spare. We are low on food, and we must get back over the mountains before summer ends.

The voyageurs would rather continue down the river. They are canoe men. Still, where Mr. Mackenzie goes, we follow. He is our leader. Tomorrow we go back upstream to the trail that we hope will take us west to the Pacific Ocean.

I am glad the Indians with us can talk to the people who live here. When they first saw us, they ran and hid. Now we get along well. They trust Mr. Mackenzie. The women are busy making moccasins for us. We certainly need them. Most of us are without shoes as a result of our hard journey through the mountains.

The explorers made many portages on their journey. Do you think they liked making portages?

What were Mackenzie's reasons for taking the Indian trail?

Before the explorers set out on the Indian trail, they built a new canoe. Then they **cached** it in the woods. They put it on a platform, bottom up, and covered it with branches to protect it from the sun. The explorers also buried some pemmican, rice and corn. Now they were ready to start walking.

Alexander Mackay's Diary
Tuesday, July 16, 1793

Why can't I manage to write in this diary more often? It's hard when you have been walking in the rain all day with a heavy pack on your back. When you finally make camp at night, all you want is to eat a good meal and then go to sleep.

We have met many Indians along the trail. Most of them are Carrier Indians. Some are going to the coast. Others are travelling to fish in the great river. They are all friendly and offer to help us.

Today we met a man and woman who gave us some fish roe to eat. First the man crushed the roe between two stones. Then he put it into some water to soak. Later his wife squeezed the roe through dried grass and put it into a birch-bark kettle filled with boiling water. She stirred it until it got thick. Then she poured fish oil over the roe and served it. Mr. Mackenzie didn't like the roe because of the oil, but I thought it was good and ate it all up.

We are surrounded by mountains again. I wonder if we will ever get through them.

Mackenzie and his men had been walking for more than 10 days. At last they saw a great mountain ahead of them. The top of it was hidden in clouds. The explorers struggled on until they came to the edge of a steep cliff. Below them they saw a wide valley filled with pine, spruce and birch trees. Through the forest wandered a broad river. The explorers followed the path down the cliff into the valley. After darkness had fallen, they came to a village beside the river.

Alexander Mackay's Diary
Thursday, July 18, 1793

*Last night we came through a **mountain pass**. Then we climbed down a steep cliff and finally came to a river. There we found a village. The Indians there welcomed us and gave us roasted salmon to eat. After we had eaten, we lay down outside under the sky and went to sleep. I have never slept so soundly in all my life.*

This morning when we awoke the Indians already had a fire going near us. They gave us a fine breakfast of roast salmon, raspberries and gooseberries. It seemed almost as if we were on holiday, sitting there by the fire eating those juicy berries.

Mackenzie and Mackay are eating berries with the Indians. Why do the explorers seem so happy?

The houses in this village are made of cedar wood. They are large and well made. Posts in the houses are carved to look like people and animals. Several families live in a house. Each family has its own fireplace and a section where it lives. The people must be very peaceful to live so close together.

Mr. Mackenzie has made friends with the chief. He will lend us two large canoes and a guide to take us down the river to the sea. The canoes are made from single cedar trees. Tomorrow we leave. I am so excited about getting to the Pacific Ocean that I don't know if I'll be able to sleep.

How have the Indians helped Mackenzie on his journey? What do you think was the most important way?

The explorers were on the Bella Coola River. The Indians they had met were called the Bella Coolas. Mackenzie and his men travelled from village to village along the river. Everywhere they went the Indians helped them.

At last the explorers came to the sea. They were at the head of a deep fiord that stretched far into the mountains. Earlier that summer Vancouver had named the fiord North Bentinck Arm. Mackenzie and his men paddled along the fiord. They were in a hurry to reach the Pacific Ocean.

Mackenzie travelled along the Bella Coola River until he reached North Bentinck Arm. How would you describe the coastline?

Page 181: Mackenzie and his men travelled along the Bella Coola River to the sea. How do you think they felt as they paddled along the river?

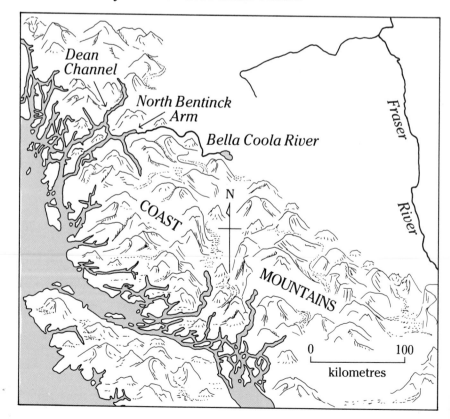

Alexander Mackay's Diary
Monday, July 22, 1793

We have finally reached the Pacific Ocean! After travelling down the river from the Indian village, we came to the head of an inlet. We stood there and stared at the ocean waves that lapped the rocky shore. At that moment I felt my heart swell with pride.

*That night we stayed at a deserted Indian village. The next morning we came down the inlet in a large canoe. Now we are camped on a large rock. We can see down a channel to the open Pacific. Mr. Mackenzie fixed our position by reading our latitude and **longitude**. Then he mixed vermilion with some grease. We all stood around him. Our hearts filled with joy and our eyes with tears as he painted these words on the rock:*

Alexander Mackenzie,
from Canada, by land,
the twenty-second of July,
one thousand seven hundred and ninety-three

The explorers have arrived at the Pacific Ocean. How can you tell from the picture that the journey was hard?

How would you have felt if you had been with Mackenzie when he reached the Pacific Ocean?

Mackenzie and his men had arrived at Dean Channel. Mackenzie didn't know it, but Vancouver had named and mapped that channel just a few weeks before.

Now Mackenzie and his men were running out of supplies. They wanted to get home before winter. They did not stop to rest. They followed the Indian trail back over the high Coast Mountains. They crossed the rolling hills to the Fraser River, where they had cached their canoe. Then they made their way back over the Great Divide to the Peace River. Once more they portaged the canoe around terrifying rapids. Then they paddled down the Peace River to the small fort from which they had started. As they approached the fort, they hoisted their flag, fired their muskets and slapped the water with their paddles. They wanted everyone to know they had returned.

Mackenzie and his men had travelled more than 3860 km in 107 days. This means they had walked and paddled about 35 km a day through some of the roughest country in the world.

Mackenzie and his men had not found a river that fur traders could take to the Pacific Ocean. Still, they had shown that it was possible to travel across Canada from the Atlantic Ocean to the Pacific Ocean.

Mackenzie's writing on the rock was washed away a long time ago. This picture shows what one artist thinks the words may have looked like. Why do you think Mackenzie wrote this message on the rock?

What Happened to Alexander Mackay?

After his great adventure with Mackenzie, Mackay went on working for the North West Company. Later he joined the Pacific Fur Company. In 1811 he sailed along the Pacific Coast on the ship *Tonquin*. No one knows exactly what happened, but Alexander Mackay was killed not far from Nootka.

What Happened to Alexander Mackenzie?

After his two great journeys, Alexander Mackenzie continued to work in the fur trade. He also published the journals of his travels, which were read in many lands. In 1802 he was made a knight by the king of England.

At last Mackenzie went back to England to live. There he married and had three children. Unfortunately, the hardships of an explorer's life had ruined his health. He died in 1820, at the age of 57.

What Have We Learned?

The explorers moved north and west across Canada. Peter Pond explored and mapped the Athabasca country. On one of his maps he showed a river flowing west from Great Slave Lake.

Alexander Mackenzie wanted to find a route to the Pacific Ocean. He thought he could reach the Pacific by going down the river that flowed out of Great Slave Lake. In 1789 he set out to find the river. On this journey, he found that the river did not flow to the Pacific Ocean. Instead, it flowed to the Arctic coast. Today that river is called the Mackenzie River.

In 1792 Mackenzie decided to try again. This time he followed the Peace River. After following many rivers and crossing many mountains, Mackenzie reached the Pacific Coast on July 22, 1793. He was the first European to prove that people could journey from the St. Lawrence River to the Pacific Ocean.

The Indians helped Mackenzie on his journeys. They acted as his guides and hunters. Mackenzie and his crew travelled in Indian canoes. They wore clothes and moccasins made by the Indian women. When fish and game were scarce, the explorers ate pemmican. Without the help of the Indians, they could not have gone very far.

Mackenzie discovered that there were many rivers and mountains between the prairies and the Pacific Coast. As a result of his journeys, Mackenzie added a vast new region to the map of Canada.

In this chapter you have learned about exploration in western Canada from 1777 to 1793.

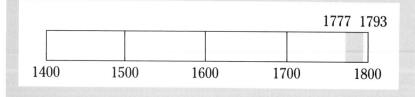

This map shows the routes of Mackenzie's two journeys. Can you name the rivers he took on each journey?

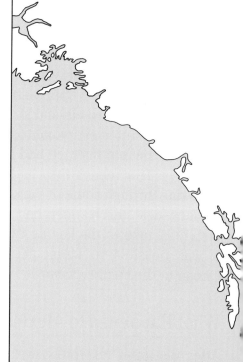

Legend

Mackenzie's journeys

1789 ——————

1792-93 — — —

PACIFIC OCEAN

184

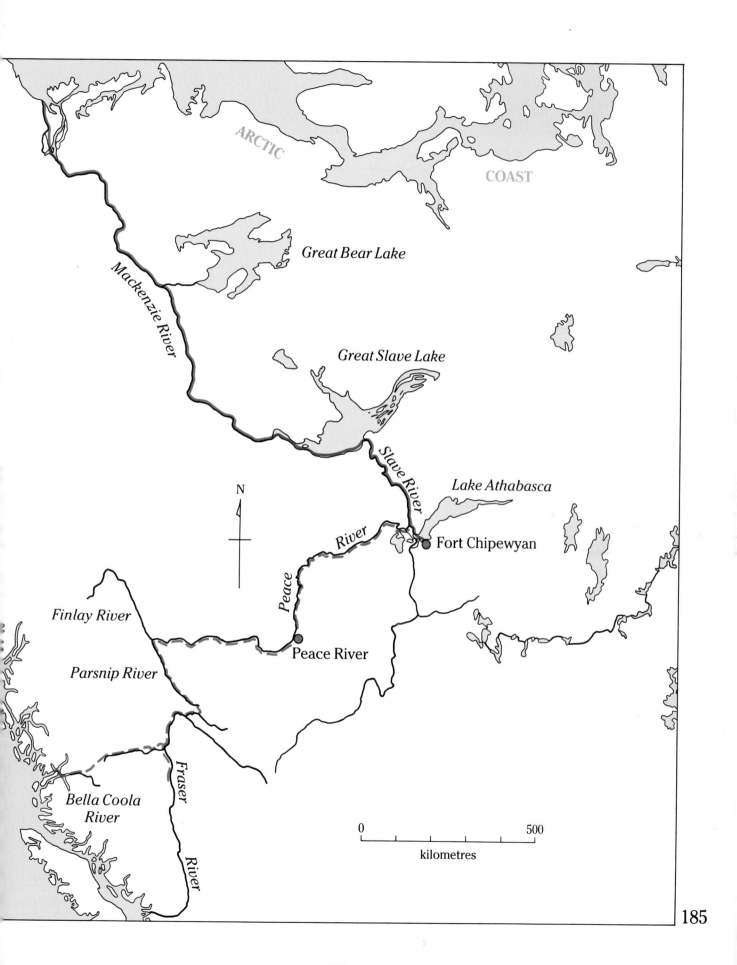

ARCTIC

COAST

Great Bear Lake

Mackenzie River

Great Slave Lake

Slave River

Lake Athabasca

River

Peace

Fort Chipewyan

Finlay River

Peace River

Parsnip River

Fraser

Bella Coola
River

River

N

0   500

kilometres

Two Points of View

When Mackenzie was exploring western Canada, he met Indians from many different tribes. One of these tribes was the Slave tribe. Another was the Bella Coola tribe. Each group welcomed the explorers in its own way. Each group made the explorers a special meal.

Northern Lights, a Slave Indian

I remember the day when strangers came to our camp. They were friendly. They gave us some wonderful gifts. We cooked a special meal of moose and caribou meat and swans' eggs. It was a delicious meal. Afterwards, we danced and sang.

How did Northern Lights and the other Slave Indians make the explorers feel welcome?
What special food did they cook for the explorers?

Raven Dawn, a Bella Coola Indian

Many years ago a small group of men visited our village. They came here from the other side of the mountains. Our chief welcomed them, and we shared a meal. The visitors liked the salmon and berries we gave them to eat. They had not eaten such good food for a long time. Then we gave the visitors soft cedar mats to sleep on for the night.

How did Raven Dawn and the other Bella Coola Indians make the explorers feel welcome?
What special food did they give the explorers?

Looking Back

Events and Feelings

Match the explorers in the first list with the feelings in the second list.

Events

a. Mackenzie and his crew left Fort Chipewyan in 1789.
b. Mackenzie reached the place where the river changes course and flows north.
c. The voyageurs cut a path around the Peace River Canyon.
d. The explorers' canoe was wrecked.
e. Mackenzie reached the Pacific Ocean.

Feelings

1. disappointed
2. hopeful
3. joyful
4. tired
5. upset

How the Indians Helped

Mackenzie took pemmican with him on both of his journeys. Write a paragraph explaining why pemmican was so important to the explorers.

Geography of the Western Mountains

Draw the outline of a mountain in the Cordillera. Use a green crayon to colour the area that is covered with coniferous trees. Use a yellow crayon to colour the area that is covered with meadows. Use a white crayon to colour the area that is covered with snow. Add a legend to explain what the colours represent.

Imagine You Were There

What would you have said or done —
if you were an Indian and the explorers arrived at your village?
if Mackenzie asked you to keep going after your canoe had smashed?
if you had been with Mackenzie when he arrived at the Pacific Ocean?

Find Out More

1. Mackenzie met many different Indian groups on his voyage to the Pacific Ocean. Pick one of the groups mentioned in this chapter. Find out about some of the customs of this group. Tell another student about these customs.
2. The Peace River Canyon looks much different today from the way it looked in 1793 when Mackenzie saw it. A large dam has been built there. Find a picture in a book or magazine of the dam on the Peace River. How does a dam change a river?
3. After Mackenzie crossed the Western Mountains, other explorers looked for a river from the mountains to the Pacific Ocean. Two of these explorers were David Thompson and Simon Fraser. Choose one of these explorers and find out more about him. Then write a paragraph about what you have learned.

7

How Was Canada Explored?

Explorers made maps wherever they went. Champlain drew this map in 1632.

Faicte l'an 1632 par le sieur de Champlain

189

Hundreds of years passed before the explorers from Europe found a way across Canada to the Pacific Ocean. At last Alexander Mackenzie wrote his name on a rock beside the Pacific Ocean. The explorers had finally travelled across Canada. They had explored from sea to sea—from the Atlantic to the Pacific.

You have followed five of these explorers on their journeys. You have learned about the hardships and the excitement of exploration. Each explorer helped you discover more about your country.

What Were the Explorers Looking For?

At first the explorers were looking for a sea route from Europe to China. They found Canada instead. Many explorers began to look for the Northwest Passage around Canada. Some explorers were also looking for things like furs and copper.

Samuel de Champlain came to Canada in 1603. Champlain wanted to find the Northwest Passage. He also wanted to build up the fur trade with the Indians. He thought it would be easier to do both these things if Europeans lived in the new land. So Champlain started a colony.

Many of the explorers were fur traders. Anthony Henday worked for the Hudson's Bay Company. In 1754 he set out across the prairies. Henday was looking for the Blackfoot Indians. He wanted the Blackfoot to bring their furs to York Factory to trade.

This time line shows when each of the five main explorers in this book explored Canada. Which two explorers were in Canada at the same time?

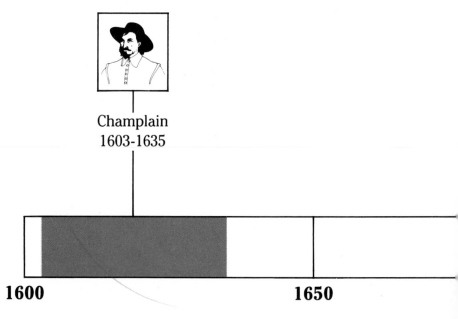

Champlain
1603-1635

1600

1650

Samuel Hearne also worked for the Hudson's Bay Company. He and the other fur traders heard about a copper mine beside a river far to the north. In 1769 Hearne set out across the Barren Grounds to look for the copper mine. Hearne also wanted to find the Northwest Passage. He hoped that the Coppermine River would be part of the Northwest Passage.

After a while explorers began to look for an entrance to the Northwest Passage along the Pacific Coast of North America. In 1791 George Vancouver sailed from England with two ships. His job was to chart the Pacific Coast and to look for an entrance to the Northwest Passage.

The explorers had begun their search for the Northwest Passage on the east coast of Canada. Slowly they moved west across the country. No one had yet reached the Pacific Ocean. In 1789 Alexander Mackenzie set out on his first journey. He was looking for a river that fur traders and their canoes could take to the Pacific Ocean.

The explorers came to Canada because they were looking for something. Some wanted to find the Northwest Passage. Others wanted to get such things as furs and copper. All the explorers wanted to find out more about the new land. Canada was an exciting place for them.

The explorers who came to Canada from Europe found furs and copper. They found out many things about Canada. None of these explorers found the Northwest Passage, however. That discovery came many years later.

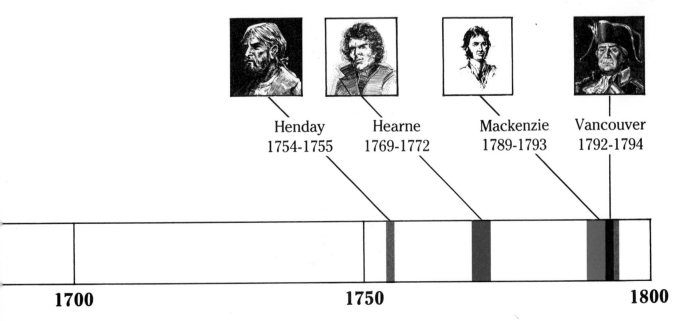

Henday
1754-1755

Hearne
1769-1772

Mackenzie
1789-1793

Vancouver
1792-1794

1700   1750   1800

The Discovery of the Northwest Passage

In the 1800s, many explorers from England sailed to the Arctic coast of Canada. They thought they would find the Northwest Passage there.

One of these explorers was John Franklin. He made three journeys to the Arctic coast. On his first two journeys, Franklin explored the coast near the Mackenzie River. In 1845, Franklin set out on his third journey. He took two ships. They were called the *Terror* and the *Erebus*. No one in England ever saw the ships or their crews again.

Other explorers tried to find the missing ships. At last Francis Leopold McClintock met some Inuit who had seen the ships and the crews. Later McClintock found messages left by two of the crew members. He also found tools and other items from the ships. From these clues, McClintock found out what happened. The *Terror* and the *Erebus* had become

John Franklin made three journeys to the Arctic coast. On his last journey, he and all his men died.

Robert McClure was the first to travel through the Northwest Passage.

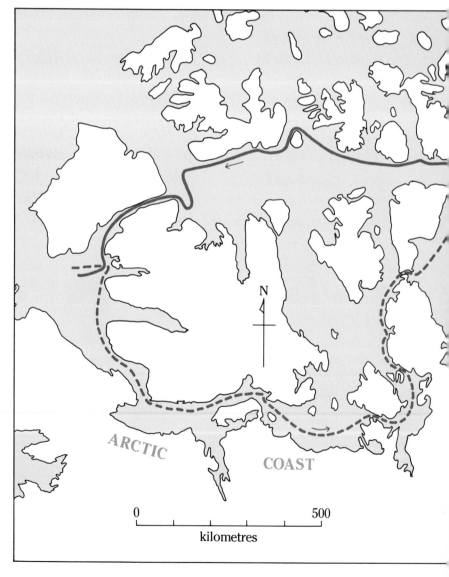

ARCTIC

COAST

0   500

kilometres

trapped in the thick ice. Then Franklin and some of the other men became ill and died. At last, the rest of the men left the ships and tried to walk to safety. They all died of cold and starvation. It was a tragic journey. But Franklin had come closer to finding the Northwest Passage than anyone before him.

Soon after, Robert McClure became the first explorer to travel through the Northwest Passage. Because of sea ice, he and his men had to leave their ship and walk part of the way. They finished the journey in another ship.

An explorer from Norway was the first to go the whole way through the Northwest Passage by ship. His name was Roald Amundsen.

The *St. Roch* was the first Canadian ship to travel through the Northwest Passage. It was also the first ship to go through the passage both ways.

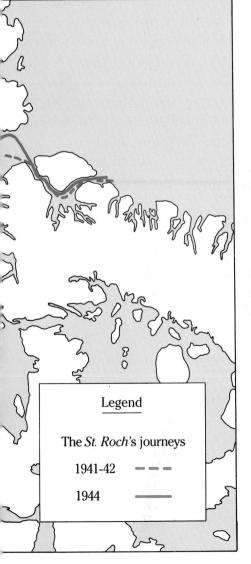

Legend

The *St. Roch*'s journeys

1941-42   - - -

1944   ———

Above: The St. Roch *travelled in both directions through the Northwest Passage.*

Left: This map shows the routes of the St. Roch *through the Northwest Passage. The ship began in the west and travelled east. On the return journey, the* St. Roch *travelled from east to west.*

How Did the Indians Help the Explorers?

Each of the explorers was helped by the Indians. The Indians had lived in Canada for a long time. Each tribe knew a lot about the country where it lived. The Indians guided the explorers through the forests, across the prairies and over the mountains. The Indians also taught the explorers how to survive in the wilderness.

When Champlain was exploring eastern Canada, his guides were the Algonquins, Montagnais and Hurons. They took Champlain up the St. Lawrence River and the Ottawa River. They showed him how to get to Georgian Bay in the land of the Hurons. The Indians also taught Champlain that a birch-bark canoe was best for exploring the rivers and lakes of Canada.

The Cree Indians guided Henday across the prairies to Blackfoot country. Henday travelled along the rivers in a birch-bark canoe made by the Cree men. A Cree woman cooked his food and made his clothes and moccasins.

Hearne travelled across the Barren Grounds with a group of Chipewyan Indians. His guide was the Chipewyan leader Matonabbee. On the journey the Chipewyan men made canoes for crossing the lakes and rivers. They also hunted caribou and buffalo for food. The Chipewyan women made warm clothes and cooked the food. They all slept in tents made from caribou skin.

Unlike the other explorers, Vancouver and his men did not depend on the Indians. They ate mostly food they had brought with them on their ships. They used European boats to explore the Pacific Coast. The explorers sometimes traded with the Indians they met, however. They often got fresh salmon from the Indians.

When Mackenzie set out to look for the river to the Pacific Ocean, several Chipewyans went with him. Like many other explorers, Mackenzie travelled in Indian canoes. He wore clothes and moccasins made by the Chipewyan women. When the hunters could not find fish or game, the explorers lived on pemmican.

The explorers from Europe had to learn the best way to explore Canada. They used the Indian methods of travel, food, shelter and clothing. Later, European explorers learned that Inuit ways were often the best for exploring the Arctic.

How the Inuit Helped the Explorers

Explorers in the Arctic learned to use Inuit food, shelter, clothing and methods of travel. The first explorer who used Inuit ways was John Ross. In 1829, Ross sailed to the Arctic to look for the Northwest Passage. His ship became locked in ice. Ross and his men spent four winters in the Arctic. While they were there, the explorers met some Inuit.

The Inuit taught Ross and his men how to make sledges and snow houses, or igloos. On hunting trips, the explorers used sledges to carry the game back to the ship. At night they slept in warm igloos.

Like the Inuit, Ross and his men ate lots of animal oil and fat. They also ate fish and seal meat. Later Ross wrote that Inuit food was the secret to surviving in the Arctic.

The explorers found that it was easy to walk on the snow in sealskin boots. They wore Inuit clothes made of caribou hide or sealskin. They slept under fur blankets.

At last Ross and his men were rescued. They could not have survived those four years in the Arctic without help from the Inuit. Later explorers also learned that the Inuit ways were best in the Arctic.

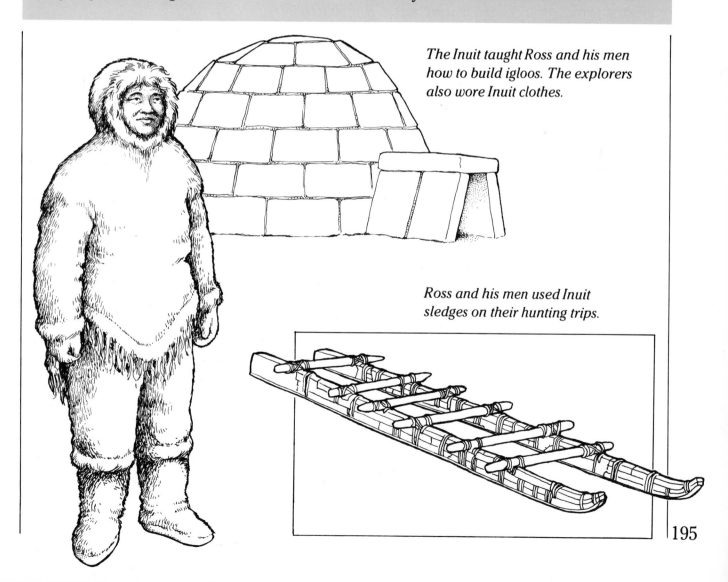

The Inuit taught Ross and his men how to build igloos. The explorers also wore Inuit clothes.

Ross and his men used Inuit sledges on their hunting trips.

195

What Did the Explorers Find Out about Canada?

As the explorers searched for the Northwest Passage, furs and copper, they learned about the geography of our country. They charted the bays, rivers, lakes and mountains. They learned about plants and animals that live in the different regions of Canada. Each explorer added another region to the map of Canada.

Champlain found out a lot about the geography of eastern Canada. He learned about the low mountains and valleys of the Appalachians. He saw the flat land of the St. Lawrence Lowland.

Henday's journey took him across part of the Interior Plains. He reached the grassy prairies of Canada. He may have seen the foothills of the Rocky Mountains. His discoveries brought the explorers one step closer to the Pacific Ocean.

Hearne travelled to the northern coast of Canada. His journey took him through part of the Canadian Shield. He travelled through forests and across the Barren Grounds. He added still another region to the map of Canada.

Vancouver charted the Pacific Coast from the northern part of present-day California to the southern part of present-day Alaska. He also named the places he explored. We use most of those names today.

On his first journey, Mackenzie went down the Mackenzie River to the Arctic coast. On his second journey, he followed many rivers and crossed many mountains until he reached the Pacific Coast. He added a vast new region, the Cordillera, to the map of Canada.

The explorers found that Canada has many geographic regions. For later explorers, there were still rivers to follow, mountains to cross and places to explore. One of these places was the Arctic.

People enjoy rafting in the rivers that flow through the Cordillera.

196

Left: Today there are many wheat farms in the southern part of the Interior Plains.

Below: The St. Lawrence Lowland is a flat region along the St. Lawrence River.

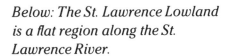

Above: Farming is important in the Appalachian region.

Above: Today you can see many log booms along the Pacific Coast.

Left: Many rivers flow through the rocky land of the Canadian Shield.

The Arctic Islands

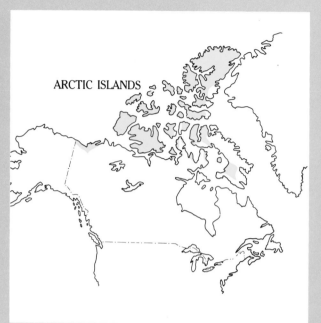

ARCTIC ISLANDS

The Arctic Islands are a large group of islands in the Arctic Ocean. The Northwest Passage goes through these islands. The pictures help you see what this region looks like today.

The islands farthest north are mountainous. The mountains are covered with glaciers and snowfields all year round. In summer, thick fog clings to the sides of the mountains for days. When the fog lifts, you might see yellow and orange lichen on the bare rock among the glaciers. No one lives on these northern islands.

People live in small villages on the islands farther south. These islands are made up of

Top: The mountains on the northern islands are covered with snow all year round.

Bottom: The islands in the south are made up of lowlands. People live in small villages on these islands.

lowlands. There the land is smooth and rounded. In winter, most parts of the islands are covered with ice and snow. The snow is dry and hard. It is easily whipped into great snowdrifts by the winter winds. The summer is short, but there are many hours of daylight. Lichens, grasses and flowers grow here. It is too cold for trees to grow in the frozen ground.

It was difficult for explorers to find a passage through the islands. The Arctic Ocean is frozen for many months of the year. Explorers' ships were sometimes frozen in the sea ice for the winter. Some ships were crushed by ice. Today, it is still hard to travel through the Northwest Passage. Icebreakers can help

ships caught in ice, though. Ships taking supplies to people who live in the north travel only in August and September.

This region has not changed much since the explorers searched for the Northwest Passage. Because it is so cold, very few people live on the Arctic Islands.

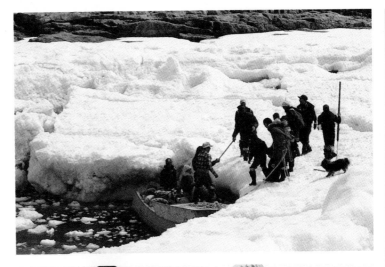

Right: In this picture you can see thick ice along the shore of one of the islands. The people are loading a canoe at the base of the ice.

Right: These Inuit children live on the Arctic Islands.

199

The End of Your Journey

You have come to the end of your journey with the explorers. You have raced down rapid-filled rivers. You have travelled across the prairies to stand at the foot of the Rocky Mountains. You have walked through forests and across the Barren Grounds to the Arctic coast. You have explored bays and inlets along the Pacific Coast. You have climbed mountains and walked over the Great Divide.

You have explored the past and reached the present. One day, you might become one of the explorers of the future.

Above: This diver is exploring the ocean. How is the diver like the other explorers you have read about?

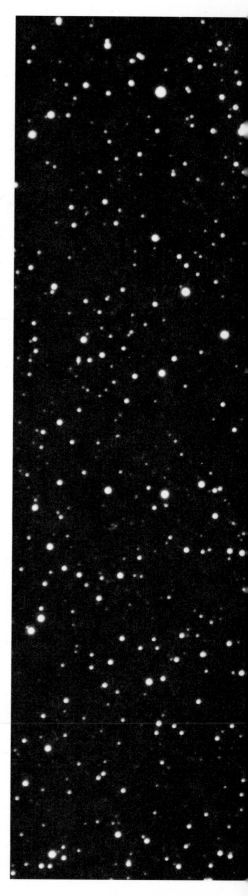

Right: This picture shows planets and stars in outer space. Do you think people will ever explore other planets?

GLOSSARY

This glossary tells you the meaning of some new words used in this book. Some of these words have other meanings, too. You will need a dictionary to find the other meanings.

The number listed after each meaning tells you the page where the word is first used. The word is in heavy print on that page.

Some of the new words are hard to say. The marks below will help you to say these words:

a	= cat	i	= it	u̇	= up
ā	= say	ī	= ride	ü	= look
e	= red	o	= dog	ū	= school
ē	= he	ō	= go	ə	= pocket
				zh	= treasure

′ is an accent mark. It points to the part of the word that you say most strongly.

jump′ ing   good bye′

Arctic Circle: an imaginary line around the earth separating the cold, northern region from the warmer, moderate region. (p. 160)

babiche (ba bēsh′): heavy thread or string made from the hides of animals. (p. 77)

barren (ba′ rən): bare, empty. Not much grows on land that is barren. (p. 42)

bay: a U-shaped body of water at a seacoast or lake shore. A bay has land on three sides. (p. 11)

beeatee (bē′ tē): a food made by filling a caribou stomach with other parts of the caribou and roasting it over a fire. (p. 100)

cache (kash): to hide something in a secret place. (p. 177)

canyon (kan′ yən): a narrow valley with steep sides, often with a river or stream at the bottom. (p. 166)

chain: several mountain ranges side by side. (p. 168)

channel: a body of water that joins two larger bodies of water; a wide strait. (p. 127)

chart: to draw a map of an area. (p. 16)

claim: to say that something belongs to you. The explorers claimed land for their countries. (p. 23)

coast: the land next to the sea; the seacoast. (p. 12)

colony: a settlement or village in a new land. (p. 30)

compass (kum′ pəs): an instrument that shows directions. (p. 158)

coniferous (ko nif′ er əs): having cones. Pines and spruces are coniferous trees. (p. 28)

continent: a very large land mass. Canada and the United States are part of the continent of North America. (p. 14)

current: the flow of the water in an ocean, a river or other body of water. (p. 140)

deciduous (də sid′ yü əs): falling off at a certain time of year. Oaks, maples and aspens are deciduous trees. (p. 45)

decoy (dē′ koi): something that looks or sounds like a bird or animal and is used to attract it. (p. 103)

divide: a ridge of land that causes the water to flow in different directions on each side. (p. 173)

downstream: down a river, moving towards the ocean. (p. 163)

fertile: able to produce crops. Plants grow well in fertile soil. (p. 45)

fiord (fē ōrd′): a long, narrow arm of the sea with steep cliffs on each side. (p. 131)

foothill: a small hill at the bottom of a mountain. (p. 82)

fork: a place where a river or a road divides into two or more parts. (p. 172)

fresh: not salty. The water in a lake or river is fresh. (p. 42)

fur trade: trading things from Europe for furs from the Indians. (p. 25)

geography (jē og′ rə fē): the different parts of the surface of the earth, including mountains, rivers, oceans, prairies, forests. (p. 16)

glacier (glā′ shər or glā′ sē ər): a large mass of ice that moves very slowly over the land. (p. 11)

governor: a person who rules or governs. (p. 110)

guide (gīd): a person who shows the way to get to a place. (p. 15)

gulf: a large bay; a part of the ocean or sea that extends far into the land. (p. 25)

harbour (har′ bər): a shelter for ships on the coast of a sea or lake. (p. 124)

iceberg: a mountain of ice floating in the ocean. Most of an iceberg is under the water. (p. 10)

ice floe: a large piece of floating ice in a river or ocean. (p. 31)

inlet: a narrow body of water that goes into the land. (p. 119)

interpreter: (in tər′ pre tər): a person who changes the words of one language into those of another language. An interpreter helps people who speak different languages to understand each other. (p. 33)

island (ī′ lənd): a piece of land with water on all sides. (p. 10)

journal (jər′ nəl): a book for writing down the events of each day. (p. 63)

latitude (lat′ i tyüd): imaginary lines running east and west around the earth. (p. 91)

legend: (lej′ ənd): a story of the past. Some legends are true, and some are only partly true. (p. 10)

lichen (lī′ kən): a small plant, somewhat like moss, that grows on trees and rocks. (p. 97)

longitude (lon′ jə tyüd *or* long′ gə tyüd): imaginary lines running north and south around the earth. (p. 182)

mainland: the major part of a continent or land mass. (p. 31)

merchant (mər′ chənt): a person who buys and sells things in order to earn money. (p. 14)

mineral: a substance that is dug out of the earth. Copper, gold and coal are examples of minerals. (p. 96)

mountain pass: a low part of land between the peaks of a mountain range. (p. 178)

mouth: the part of a river or stream that joins another body of water, such as a lake or ocean. (p. 31)

muskeg: a bog or swamp of soft, spongy moss and water. (p. 97)

navigation (nav ə gā′ shən): the act of steering or guiding a ship or boat on its proper course. (p. 127)

Northwest Passage (nōrth′ west pas′ ij): a way to get from the Atlantic Ocean to the Pacific Ocean by sea. The Northwest Passage is along the northern coast of North America. (p. 14)

pemmican (pem′ i kən): a food made from dried meat, ground to a powder and mixed with hot fat. Sometimes berries are added to pemmican. (p. 155)

portage (pōr tazh′): the carrying of boats and goods over the land. People make portages around dangerous parts of a river or from one body of water to another. (p. 34)

prairie: a large area of flat or rolling land with grass but few or no trees. In Canada, the prairies stretch across the provinces of Alberta, Saskatchewan and Manitoba. (p. 8)

quadrant (kwod′ rənt): an instrument that helps people find their position on earth. (p. 91)

range: a row of mountains. (p. 28)

rapids: a dangerous part of a river where the water moves very quickly over rocks. (p. 15)

reef: a line of rocks or sand near the surface of the water. (p. 139)

region (rē′ jən): a large part of the surface of the earth; a large area. (p. 16)

route (rūt): a way to travel to another place. A route may be along a path, road, river or ocean. (p. 14)

saga (sag′ ə): a long story or legend about important events in the past told by the people of Iceland, Sweden, Norway and Denmark. (p. 12)

sagamité (sa ga′ mē tā): an Indian food made by boiling powdered corn in water. Sometimes fish or meat is added to the sagamité. (p. 42)

scurvy: a disease caused by not eating enough vitamin C. Explorers got scurvy because they did not get enough vitamin C from fruit and vegetables. (p. 26)

sinew (sin′ yū): a strong cord that holds bone and muscle together. (p. 76)

site: the place or position of something. (p. 33)

slough (slū): a body of water that forms when ice melts or rain collects. (p. 69)

sound: a long, narrow body of water. Sometimes a sound joins two larger bodies of water and sometimes it is a narrow inlet in the coast. (p. 125)

strait: a narrow body of water that joins two larger bodies of water. (p. 119)

tide: the rise and fall of the level of the ocean, which happens about twice a day. (p. 127)

trading post: a building where a trading company has set up a store. (p. 54)

tree line: the point where trees will no longer grow. It is too cold for trees to grow beyond the tree line. (p. 97)

tundra: flat land in the north where trees cannot grow. (p. 97)

upstream: up a river, going away from the ocean. (p. 162)

voyageur (voi ə zhər′): a French-Canadian who paddled the canoes and explored for the fur trading companies. (p. 57)

weir (wēr): a fence made with branches or stakes set in a river or stream to catch fish. (p. 139)

INDEX

This index will help you to find information in this book. Topics are listed in alphabetical order. Some of the topics are then divided into subtopics.

Page numbers are listed after the topic or subtopic. If you turn to the pages listed after a certain topic, you will find information about it.

Some page numbers are in heavy print. This means there is a map on that page that relates to the topic.

Explorations A Canadian Social Studies Program for Elementary Schools

Acknowledgements

Commissioned Illustrations
Fred Forster: Chapter 6; front cover.
Nola Johnston: Chapters 2 and 7.
Brent Lynch: Chapters 3 and 5; back cover.
Rich Symmers: Chapter 4.
Maps
Karen Ewing
Amely Jurgenliemk
Cartographic Consultant
Bob Galois
Photographs and Other Illustrations
Carolyn Angus: pp. 130-131, centre.
Fred Bruemmer: p. 199, top right.
Fred Chapman/Photo/Graphics: p. 68, top;
p. 69, top; p. 97, bottom right; p. 131, top; p.
169, bottom right; pp. 196-197, top; p. 197,
bottom right.
City of Bristol Museum & Art Gallery: p. 24
— *Departure of Cabot.*
Confederation Life Collection: pp. 12-13 —
The Vikings by Jerry Lazare; p. 56, top —
Kelsey on the Plains by Rex Woods; p. 121,
top — *Captain George Vancouver, R.N.* by
J. D. Kelly; p. 148 — *Early Fur Traders* by
J. D. Kelly.
A. D. Dickson/Image Finders: p. 19, bottom;
pp. 146-147.
Koos Dykstra/Image Finders: pp. 132-133.
Environment Canada, Canadian Forestry
Service, pp. 198-199, top.
John Foster/Masterfile: pp. 94-95.
Glenbow Museum: p. 9 — *On the Move* by
Gerald Tailfeathers; pp. 156-157, bottom —
photograph by J. Garner; p. 177 — *A
Portage* by John Innes.

Brenda Guild, Department of Fisheries &
Oceans: p. 139, top right.
Bob Herger/Photo/Graphics: p. 131, bottom;
p. 168, left; p. 168, right.
J. A. Kraulis/Photo/Graphics: p. 45, bottom
right; p. 96, left; p. 181.
Roger Laurilla/Photo/Graphics: p. 55.
Dave Looy/Image Finders: p. 67.
Wayne Lynch/Photo/Graphics: p. 19, second
from top; pp. 52-53; p. 56, bottom.
Neil McDaniel: p. 200, left.
Alan McOnie/Image Finders: p. 19, third
from top; pp. 86-87.
Mary Evans Picture Gallery, London: p. 22.
Gunter Marx/Photo/Graphics: p. 19, second
from bottom; pp. 116-117; p. 127.
Ben Mayer/Hansen Planetarium:
pp. 200-201.
Frank Mayrs/Image Finders: pp. 198-199,
bottom.
Pat Morrow/Photo/Graphics: p. 68, bottom;
p. 79; p. 95, right.
National Map Collection, Public Archives
Canada: pp. 6-7; pp. 188-189.
NFB/Photothèque: p. 97, top right —
photograph by George Hunter; pp. 198-199,
top — photograph by Scot Miller and David
Hiscocks.
Parks Canada: p. 193.
Gerald Perreault/Image Finders: pp. 44-45,
top; pp. 196-197, centre.
Provincial Archives of British Columbia: p.
119 (28220); p. 125 (289); p. 151, left (100).
Public Archives Canada: p. 5, top (C-773); p.
14 (C-69711); p. 26, bottom (C-6680) — *The

First Prescription in Canada, 1536* by C. W.
Jefferys; p. 32 (C-98232) — *The Order of
Good Cheer, 1606* by C. W. Jefferys; p. 57
(C-2773) — *Voyageurs at Dawn* by Frances
Hopkins; p. 60 (C-70247) — *The Brothers La
Vérendrye in Sight of the Western
Mountains, New Year's Day, 1743* by C. W.
Jefferys; p. 73 (C-22276) — *Henday Enters
the Blackfoot Camp, 1754* by F. Arbuckle; p.
107 (C-70250) — *Samuel Hearne on His
Journey to the Coppermine, 1770* by C. W.
Jefferys; p. 157, right (C-16415) — *The
Voyageurs Camp* by Alf. Sandham; p. 182
(C-73712) — *Mackenzie at the Pacific* by
C. W. Jefferys; p. 192, top (C-5150) — *John
Franklin* by Negelen; p. 192, bottom
(C-87256) — *Sir Robert McClure* after
S. Pearce, 1855.
S. Roberts/Image Finders: p. 141.
Denis A. St-Onge: pp. 100-101.
Robert Semeniuk: p. 199, bottom right.
Lloyd Sutton/Photo/Graphics: p. 169, top
right.
University Library, Heidelberg: p. 10.
Jürgen Vogt/Photo/Graphics: p. 19, top; pp.
20-21; p. 28, left; p. 28, bottom right; pp.
28-29, top; p. 29, bottom left; p. 29, bottom
right; p. 44, left; pp. 44-45, bottom; p. 58; pp.
164-165; p. 197, top right; p. 197, bottom
left.
Richard Wright/Photo/Graphics: p. 69,
bottom left; p. 69, bottom right; p. 72; p.
130, left; pp. 168-169, centre; p. 196, bottom
right.